Stepping into Administration

How to Succeed in Making the Move

Thomas A. Kersten

ROWMAN & LITTLEFIELD EDUCATION
A division of
ROWMAN & LITTLEFIELD PUBLISHERS, INC.
Lanham • New York • Toronto • Plymouth, UK

Published by Rowman & Littlefield Education
A division of Rowman & Littlefield Publishers, Inc.
A wholly owned subsidiary of The Rowman & Littlefield Publishing Group, Inc.
4501 Forbes Boulevard, Suite 200, Lanham, Maryland 20706
http://www.rowmaneducation.com

Estover Road, Plymouth PL6 7PY, United Kingdom

Copyright © 2010 by Thomas Kersten

All rights reserved. No part of this book may be reproduced in any form or by any
electronic or mechanical means, including information storage and retrieval systems,
without written permission from the publisher, except by a reviewer who may quote
passages in a review.

British Library Cataloguing in Publication Information Available

Library of Congress Cataloging-in-Publication Data

Kersten, Thomas.
  Stepping into administration : how to succeed in making the move / Thomas Kersten.
      p. cm.
  Includes bibliographical references and index.
  ISBN 978-1-60709-618-4 (cloth : alk. paper) — ISBN 978-1-60709-619-1 (pbk. : alk.
paper) — ISBN 978-1-60709-595-8 (electronic)
  1. Educational leadership. 2. School management and organization. I. Title.

LB2805.K445 2010
  371.20023—dc22   2010012725

∞ ™ The paper used in this publication meets the minimum requirements of
American National Standard for Information Sciences—Permanence of Paper
for Printed Library Materials, ANSI/NISO Z39.48-1992.

Printed in the United States of America

Contents

Preface: Considering a Career in School Administration

$\mathcal{A}$s I think back to the spring of my senior year in college, I can still vividly remember how excited I was when I landed my first teaching position. At the time, teaching positions were scarce as school enrollments were in decline and schools of education were graduating more certified teachers than available positions. Yet, even at the beginning of my first year of teaching, I was already thinking about my future. One of my earliest memories is wondering whether I would ultimately move into higher education or become a school administrator.

You might wonder why any beginning teacher would even have such a thought. That is a valid question, and one that might apply to most novices—but not everyone. I wouldn't be surprised if a certain percentage of ambitious individuals, particularly the type who seek leadership experiences, were already thinking about next steps.

The answer to my question, in fact, emerged within a couple of years of teaching. After researching my graduate school options, I discovered that I could complete my master's degree in English, which would open up the possibility of pursuing my doctorate in English and focusing my career in academia. I learned that I could earn my administrative certification after completing my master's. As a result, I began my graduate program during my first year of teaching, which ultimately allowed me to advance on the salary schedule and kept my administrative career options open. I also decided that this would give me a good opportunity to observe my principal and assistant principal, to help me consider whether school administration was for me.

As I think back on those years, I don't know whether it was the fact that I taught in a comprehensive, well-run suburban district or the fact that I worked for highly motivated and effective administrators, but I found myself extremely interested in an administrative career. Yes, I saw the stress they were under and listened as staff regularly questioned administrative decisions or challenged their authority, but the lure of leadership and the flexibility I saw in their day-to-day responsibilities attracted me.

As I was about to complete my English degree, I decided to discuss my interest in administration with my principal and ask for his advice. He did what so many effective administrators do. He described what a great career choice he had made. As was consistent with his upbeat personality and unwavering enthusiasm, he motivated and encouraged me. It was at this moment that I decided that school administration was where I really wanted to be.

Later the next school year, I asked for suggestions on how I could gain some administrative experience. As the savvy principal he was, he recognized an opportunity to tap me for several leadership-related, management tasks in our school. One of the first was to serve as chair for the North Central accreditation process. At the time, I remember him explaining to me with a sense of pride that we were going to be one of the first junior high schools in Illinois to seek accreditation.

He also put me in charge of our school's unique student activity program. As part of the initial movement to a middle school philosophy, with its focus on student-centered instructional and enrichment activities, we shortened classes once a week, creating a special end-of-the-day activity period. Faculty members were responsible for developing unique student clubs, sports, and other experiences, from which students chose the ones that most interested them.

Both the North Central process and student activities responsibilities gave me my first real sense of administration. While I was a highly motivated, career-oriented person, I learned quickly that a good portion of the faculty had little, if any, interest in either the accreditation process or the activity program. They saw both as unnecessary busywork that just added to their daily responsibilities. They were quick to use "lounge time" to let their feelings be known. Even though I became the point person for both, fortunately I was not the principal who was responsible for dealing with marginally motivated faculty members. However, I did benefit from the opportunity to observe his management style.

The principal also assigned me responsibility for before school outside supervision, including serving as our liaison with the bus drivers. Here I was—willing to volunteer to stand outside every day, in all types of Chicago weather, for twenty minutes before the school doors opened, as the only supervisor for over eight hundred seventh and eighth graders as they arrived at school! As I think back on this experience, I realize I learned a great deal about managing students, winning the support of school support personnel, and communication. Needless to say, these administrative responsibilities were great learning experiences.

During that school year, our assistant principal suffered from appendicitis. Since he was expected to be out for a couple of weeks, the principal asked me if I would be willing to serve in his absence for a few days. I was so excited. I would be released from my teaching duties, have no set schedule, and work out of the assistant principal's office. Now, I thought, I would really find out what it was like to be an administrator.

In my newfound role as Assistant to the Principal, the title the principal assigned me, I thought I was truly starting to understand administration. Here I was, doing what real administrators did. In reality, I spent most of my time either walking the halls, sitting in the office looking at files, or supervising the lunchroom. During this time, only one student was sent to my office—merely for laughing in class. What I didn't realize was that staff members were basically ignoring me because the assistant wasn't there. Nonetheless, I concluded that I could handle the responsibilities of the assistant principal's role quite easily, and I became extremely motivated to find my first position.

After I completed my certification, I soon had my opportunity. I was hired as an assistant principal in a neighboring school district. I began in mid-August and quickly became enmeshed in tasks such as managing the student registration process and assisting the principal in preparing for opening-day school activities and the first faculty meeting. I couldn't have been more excited. I was now an administrator.

Then the first day of school arrived. I was very busy meeting buses and greeting students, staff, and parents, when something magical occurred. The bell for homeroom rang and everyone disappeared into their classrooms. Here I was, standing in the hallway with the principal, with nothing specific to do. For the first time in my career, I did not have a class to teach. So I decided to go to the faculty lounge for a cup of coffee. Wow, wasn't administration amazing?

Well, this thrill lasted one more day. Shortly thereafter, I began my "real" career in school administration as teachers started to send students to my office for class tardiness, talking in class, and not completing homework. Their basic expectation was that I assign each student a detention, and then supervise them in detention hall after school, which I did four days a week. There were no problem-solving conversations or collaborative meetings with the teachers and students. Rather, the focus was strictly punishment, and I was the head punisher.

Before long, I realized that as an assistant principal I had very few free minutes for myself. Until this moment, I had never understood how many

staff and teachers have problems with students and parents and expect someone else to exercise the wisdom of Solomon to solve them. Up to that point,
I'd only had my personal experiences upon which to draw. In my few years
teaching, I'd only once had to escort a student to the assistant principal, and
even in that instance, the three of us worked it through together.

By Thanksgiving, my head was spinning. I had thought that I had a reasonable understanding of the role of the assistant principal. Remember, I had
been an active, involved, and dedicated teacher who had been the Assistant
to the Principal. Why didn't I have a clue about what administrators actually
do, how they would have managed the challenges I initially faced, or how I
could have minimized the administrative learning curve? What I finally realized is that you cannot completely understand administration until you are an
administrator. However, I also recognized that even though you do not fully
understand all the realities of school administration, with certain knowledge
and skills, you can be better prepared for your first administrative position.

As I moved through my early administrative years, I continued to
discover how little I knew about effective administration. Even though my
instincts were good, I kept stumbling, but fortunately not too badly. I realized that if I had had a broader perspective and understood some of the basic
principles of effective school-based leadership, not just in theory, but also
in practice, I might have avoided some of the consternation and missteps I
experienced.

This book, *Stepping into Administration: How to Succeed in Making the
Move*, is written to share important information that novice administrators
can use to soften the initial learning curve and make the transition more
smoothly from teaching to their first administrative positions.

Acknowledgments

$\mathcal{I}$ can truly attest to the fact that no published book is solely the work of a single author. Rather, a book such as this, moves from a series of ideas to print only with the assistance and support of some very important people. I am indebted to several individuals in particular whose personal contributions of time and professional expertise helped make this book a reality.

First and foremost is my wonderful wife Beth. Throughout this project, not only did she encourage me every step of the way, but as a school administrator herself, she offered valuable insights, advice, and critical feedback which shaped the structure and content of the final product. No matter how busy or overworked she was at any given moment, she was always there for me.

In addition, I am indebted to my good friend and colleague, Nelson Armour, who was a valuable peer reviewer. Over the years, he has generously given of his time and expertise whether I was preparing a journal article or writing a book. As a highly experienced and successful public school administrator, his contributions were invaluable. Most important, I appreciated his honest and direct assessment of whatever I had written and his willingness to offer his professional insights.

Also, I want to thank my friend Lee Rosch who volunteered to edit the manuscript. Although Lee's background is in finance, he has a special interest in and talent for editing. I was happy to accept his offer. As an independent critic, Lee provided not only valuable technical editing assistance, but the perspective of an outside observer. He brought a reality perspective to the manuscript that only someone from outside the world of education could.

Finally, I want to acknowledge three school administrators who reviewed key chapters of the book: Jac McBride, Director of Special Services, Skokie School District 68; Lea Anne Frost, Director of Instruction, Special Education District of Lake County; and Megan Hernandez, Principal of John Jay Elementary School in Elk Grove School District 59. Their knowledge in specialized areas contributed greatly to the final product.

Preparing for a Career in Administration

*H*ave you ever served as a member of an interview committee composed of teachers, parents, administrators, and support staff who were part of the selection process for an assistant principal or principal? If you have, you know that the decades-old tradition of promoting the male physical education teacher / coach is long gone. In fact, candidates who do not have content-area teaching backgrounds often find themselves at a distinct disadvantage.

Consider for a moment how an interview committee might respond to an elementary principal candidate who was a high school physical education instructor. What do you think would be the focus of the committee's conversation after the interview?

Unlike in the 1950s, the 1960s, and even the 1970s, when an administrator's success was often judged on whether he or she "ran a tight ship," including staying on top of student discipline, principals today are expected to be knowledgeable and articulate on an array of curriculum and instructional issues. Good management is just a given.

Candidates such as the physical education teacher face a significant uphill battle convincing teachers and parents that they have the knowledge of curriculum and best educational practices to be highly effective instructional leaders. Remember that administrators are not hired to be school or district managers. Rather, they are expected to provide leadership for school improvement.

In the above example, many committee members would immediately disqualify the high school candidate: first, for a lack of elementary experience; and, second, because they would assume the teacher lacked a strong understanding of regular classroom instruction. Parents might also question the person's ability to lead new initiatives and improve the school. In reality, these candidates would probably be eliminated from consideration during the applicant screening process.

The high school teacher scenario should not discourage candidates from non-regular classroom backgrounds from considering a career in administration. Rather, I present it in order to illustrate how much more knowledgeable school administrators are expected to be today than they ever were before. All candidates, whether they have experiences in traditional classroom settings, teach in special areas, or serve in support roles, must develop a strong, up-to-date understanding of the latest practices, issues, and trends in the field.

However, before exploring how to build your professional knowledge base, a brief look at what research tells us about the role of the principal is useful.

LEADERS MAKE A DIFFERENCE

Principals do make a difference. Even forty years ago, if you had asked almost anyone associated with K–12 education if principals made a difference, the answer would have been "of course." People just intuitively believe this. Most probably feel that they can differentiate between an effective and ineffective principal. However, the difference today is that there is a growing body of research that is confirming the positive impact effective principals can have on increasing student achievement and improving schools (Darling-Hammond et al., 2007; Marzano, Waters, and McNulty, 2005; Murphy, 2002; Schmoker, 2001; Davis et al., 2005; Leithwood et al., 2004).

Educational administration professors often incorporate into their class discussions an activity in which students are asked to describe the most and least effective principals or assistant principals with whom they have ever worked. Talk about a discussion starter! Although they describe both, invariably the conversation centers on the ineffective. Everyone seems to know what poor performers do or do not do. However, more often than not, they have more difficulty describing what makes an effective building-level leader.

Some principals are extremely effective leaders. They represent the type of administrator who ensures that every system in the school operates smoothly and effectively. Their teachers never consider for a moment the possibility that anything about the school would be disorganized. Student and staff schedules are prepared in a timely fashion, meetings are well planned, everyone knows when and where activities are scheduled, student lunchroom procedures flow smoothly, and special activities such as award ceremonies, open house, parent conferences, and graduation are flawlessly managed.

In addition, these principals have such strong management skills that the operation of the school appears seamless. Unlike in some schools, teachers do not need to worry that they will hear about a school assembly scheduled for that day from students rather than the principal! As a result of the principal's organizational skills, faculty members can focus on their teaching responsibilities rather than worry about day-to-day management issues.

Beyond the management dimension, highly effective principals are adept instructional leaders, many of them having exhibited this skill even before the term became indigenous in educational jargon. They know how to develop focused school goals and how to raise just the right questions to stimulate reflective thinking. Often they are fixtures in the hallways and classrooms, as well as adept communicators. Their teachers typically believe that they teach in a "flagship" school, but they might not be able to identify any specific research to support their impressions of effective school level leadership.

SCHOOL LEADERSHIP RESEARCH

Over the years, a variety of leadership theories have been proposed to attempt to explain educational leadership behavior. These theories have been subject to continuous research, which has begun to reveal what it is that effective leaders do that is particularly linked to increasing student achievement. Through a meta-analysis of sixty-nine research studies, three researchers, Marzano, Waters, and McNulty (2005), identified "The Twenty-One Responsibilities of the School Leader" (41–64) that are positively correlated with student achievement. These are summarized in table 1.1.

Their work highlights how critically important it is for aspiring administrators to understand what is known about effective school leadership. No longer is trial and error an acceptable approach to educational leadership, especially as research-based evidence of what really works mounts. For a more thorough understanding of each of these responsibilities, you will want to read their book, *School Leadership that Works: From Research to Results* (Marzano, Waters, and McNulty, 2005).

You will note that Marzano, Waters, and McNulty (2005) identify "knowledge of curriculum, instruction, and assessment practices" as an important factor in effective leadership, listing it as one of the twenty-one responsibilities. As aspiring administrators, you must begin to develop your professional knowledge base during your teaching years rather than after you enter administration.

Table 1.1. Twenty-one responsibilities correlated with student academic achievement

Responsibility	Definition (the extent to which the principal . . .)
Affirmation	Recognizes and celebrates accomplishments and acknowledges failures
Change agency	Is willing to challenge and actively challenges the status quo
Contingent rewarding	Recognizes and rewards individual accomplishments
Communication	Establishes strong lines of communication with and among teachers and students
Culture	Fosters shared beliefs and a sense of community and cooperation
Discipline	Protects teachers from issues and influences that would detract from their teaching time and focus
Flexibility	Adapts his or her leadership behavior to the needs of the current situation and is comfortable with dissent
Focus	Establishes clear goals and keeps those goals in the forefront of the school's attention
Ideals/beliefs	Communicates and operates from strong ideals and beliefs about schooling
Input	Involves teachers in the design and implementation of important decisions and policies
Intellectual stimulation	Ensures that faculty and all staff are aware of the most current theories and practices and makes the discussion of these a regular aspect of the school's culture
Involvement in curriculum, instruction, and assessment	Is directly involved in the design and implementation of curriculum, instruction, and assessment practices
Knowledge of curriculum, instruction, and assessment practices	Is knowledgeable about current curriculum, instruction, and assessment practices
Monitoring/evaluating	Monitors the effectiveness of school practices and their impact on student learning
Optimizing	Inspires and leads new and challenging innovations
Order	Establishes a set of standard operating procedures and routines
Outreach	Is an advocate and spokesperson for the school to all stakeholders
Relationships	Demonstrates an awareness of the personal aspects of teachers and staff
Resources	Provides teachers with the professional development necessary for the successful execution of their jobs
Situational awareness	Is aware of the details and undercurrents in the running of the school and uses this information to address current and potential problems
Visibility	Has quality contact and interactions with teachers and students

DEVELOPING YOUR ADMINISTRATIVE KNOWLEDGE BASE

Many administrators, including those who are assistant principals as well as elementary and middle school principals, discover after they assume their initial leadership positions how little they have taken advantage of their time as teachers to prepare for their administrative careers.

Young teachers' professional lives usually revolve around graduate school and classroom teaching. Anything that does not lead to completing graduate school course work or contribute immediately to teaching is relegated to the back of the mind. At the early stages of their careers, the primary goal is to be at least a good enough teacher to earn tenure. After that, if they aspire to careers in educational administration, the focus shifts to anything that may help land that first administrative position. In essence, because of their ambition to become administrators, they might never fully explore how to be outstanding teachers.

This oversight becomes very apparent during their initial years in administration. Novice administrators often find themselves enmeshed in a broad range of professional development activities, both within their school districts and through conferences and workshops. As teachers, they probably attended institute day activities, which were at times peripherally related to their teaching assignments. Some were also generally unaware that outside workshop or conference opportunities existed. Now, as administrators, they begin to recognize what they never knew was available.

Back in the 1970s, it was not uncommon for administrators to find themselves enmeshed in whatever issues were the educational topic du jour. One of the most prominent was a new approach referred to as the *lesson design model*, which was popularized by the renowned researcher Madeline Hunter.

This model became so popular that school district administrators and teachers throughout the country were finding themselves "Hunterized"—that is, trained in Hunter's instructional planning model. In many school districts, administrators attended additional workshops similar in content, and met as an administrative team for hours to plan how to integrate lesson design into classroom instruction—all without teacher involvement.

It was not uncommon in some school districts for portions of administrative team meetings to be devoted to discussions and even debates about educational methods or curriculum models. At times, the pace of these new ideas may even have seemed overwhelming, but the information was more often professionally stimulating. Administrators found themselves learning more about the field than ever before, with many becoming very adept at explaining and discussing trends and best practices.

Once empowered with new knowledge, these administrators were expected to devise ways to infuse the lesson design model into the fabric of their schools. What some administrators probably realized was that they were privy to a vast amount of information which, because they were no longer teachers, they could not actually "test" in their classrooms. This was an important lesson for some administrators, who realized that those who could most benefit from staff development were actually the last to receive it.

The lesson design experience highlights the importance of recognizing the value of building your personal professional knowledge base when you are still a classroom teacher rather than waiting until you enter administration. Consider for a moment how much more effective you could be as a teacher or beginning administrator, if you had the opportunity to test in your classroom what you learned during your graduate school coursework and professional development workshops.

As you are considering a career in administration, a question you need to ask yourself is, what can I do during my teaching years to ensure that I am an up-to-date, knowledgeable school leader? Below are several strategies you might want to consider.

Strategy 1: Learn as much as you can as quickly as you can.

Beginning teachers and those in graduate school programs must make a significant paradigm shift in their priorities. Instead of focusing on "How can I earn my degree as quickly and painlessly as possible?" or "How can I best survive this teaching day?" you must ask yourself, "How can I maximize my professional learning?" When your thought process shifts to learning rather than surviving, you open up endless avenues for professional growth.

One simple way to enhance your background is to increase your professional reading. For example, with the explosion of information on the Web, you can easily research topics, as well as registering for Web-based newsletters and forums which discuss an array of important topics and issues in the field. You should also seek out workshops and seminars of interest. You can ask your principal to support your attendance. If this is not an option, consider those that are offered after school or on weekends.

Strategy 2: Think of your classroom as a research lab.

Teachers know that to a large extent their classrooms are their private domains. In fact, the reason many choose teaching as a career is that they relish the thought of being their own "classroom bosses." Since time immemorial, teachers have closed their doors and made decisions about what and how they teach. Staff developers often point out that teachers regularly make hundreds of decisions daily, noting that those who make the best decisions are the most successful. This may or may not be research based, but most teachers find that it resonates.

Too often teachers close their minds to new ideas and revert back to what they have done in the past. How often have you heard a colleague say, "We tried that years ago and it did not work"? The reality is that they may have heard something about a particular approach but did very little, if anything, to understand and apply it. In education, teachers, in general, are very skeptical of educational research and tend to resist research-based change unless they are really convinced it will improve what they do in their classrooms.

As an aspiring administrator, you have the opportunity to break from this mold and use your teaching time to take what you have learned and apply it in your classroom. To illustrate this, consider the following example. At the moment, one of the "hot topics" is response to intervention (RtI). A certain percentage of veteran teachers probably see it as nothing more than the reincarnation of a pupil personnel team process designed to shift the responsibility for a student's lack of progress to them. Others think that it is merely a popularized attempt to reduce special educational enrollments and save dollars by blocking easy access to special education services through a series of required prereferral interventions.

For prospective administrators, RtI offers a potentially powerful learning opportunity. As a learner, you should view this as an opportunity to understand RtI theory and how you can apply it to your teaching. If you take this approach, not only will you become articulate on the topic, but you will begin to understand its efficacy for classroom instruction. In addition, since you will now be up-to-date in the field and able to explain how you implemented RtI, you will enhance your viability as an administrative candidate.

Strategy 3: Show initiative.

Many people have talent and intelligence but fail to make full use of their abilities in life. What is the reason? Often the answer is a lack of initiative. Those who display a sense of curiosity, seek out learning opportunities, and recognize potential in different situations are often most successful in whatever they attempt. If you, too, want to stand out in the administrative candidate pool and increase your administrative marketability, you should be the type of person who demonstrates initiative both outside and inside the school district.

Not that many years ago, educators were introduced to a phenomenon called the Internet. Because it was so new and outside the experiences of many teachers and administrators, most educators initially avoided this technology. In fact, at first, a substantial portion of teachers and administrators were even unsure how to boot up a computer. Computer literacy workshops became the rage.

While most educators took a "wait and see" attitude, some recognized the entrepreneurial potential of technology. They saw that most teachers and many administrators were reticent about computers and the emerging Internet. Rather than view this as an insurmountable challenge, they saw it as an opportunity. Those few, some of whom had little more knowledge about technology that the typical educator, used their entrepreneurial skills to create seminars on topics such as "Introduction to the Internet," through which they taught teachers about the Internet itself and how to access it easily.

What was amazing was that these entrepreneurs often knew little more about the Internet than their workshop attendees. However, they understood how to market their programs and deliver them well. Some even partnered with local universities that provided graduate school credit. In any event, they made sure that the workshops were well paced and easy to understand. Today, what was discussed would be considered extremely elementary, but at the time, teachers found it eye-opening. Successes such as this demonstrate the power of personal initiative.

You too should look for opportunities to take initiative in your own school or school district. Most school administrators would relish faculty members who volunteered to serve on school or district staff development committees. These not only let your district administrators get to know you, but expand your understanding of how to work effectively in group collaborative planning, especially with other grade levels or different content areas.

As a member of a staff development committee, you will interact with teachers and administrators, plan staff development, and undoubtedly even have a chance to be a presenter. These types of experiences teach you how to lead initiatives, as well as providing valuable experience working with adults, which is what administrators do.

Also, within the school district, aspiring administrators can enhance their own knowledge by recognizing that new experiences can be opportunities rather than obstacles. This may be as simple as demonstrating initiative at the school or district level. When committees are formed or calls are made for volunteers, you should consider these situations as learning opportunities through which you can not only show your initiative but also demonstrate to others, including staff and administrators, that you have the knowledge, desire, and drive to lead.

Strategy 4: Become active in professional organizations.

Look at many administrative resumes and you will find a section titled something like "Professional Memberships." One way to build relationships and create professional networks, all while learning more about our field, is to join professional associations.

This is actually quite simple. One association you can join as a teacher is the Association for Supervision and Curriculum Development (ASCD). For less than one hundred dollars, your annual membership will include a monthly journal, free books on hot topics, a newsletter delivered as a daily e-mail, and access to workshops and conferences. By just reading these materials, you can substantially enhance your understanding of any number of educational topics.

You could also consider membership in your state and national principal associations, such as the National Association of Elementary School Principals or the National Association of Secondary School Principals. They offer member benefits similar to those provided by ASCD. Some even have a membership category for aspiring members.

SUMMARY

One of the keys to landing your first administrative position and getting off to a good start in your career is building a strong personal knowledge base. This begins during your first years as a classroom teacher and continues through your graduate school educational leadership preparation program. The more you learn about the things highly effective principals do to increase student achievement and the latest trends, issues, and best practices in the field, the greater the likelihood that you will successfully navigate the administrator selection process and land your first position. You will also avoid some of the initial pitfalls beginning administrators typically encounter, and increase the likelihood of successfully accelerating your personal learning curve.

· 2 ·

Making the Most of
Your First Few Weeks

$\mathcal{A}$bsolutely essential skills for administrative success are management and communication. Everyone expects administrators to possess the organizational and communication skills necessary to ensure that the day-to-day operation of the school is seamless. In fact, teachers, parents, support staff, and students want school administrators who will not only ensure that the school runs well but who will be effective communicators.

However, if the school is not well managed, then increased miscommunication with staff and parents, a sense of schoolwide disequilibrium, and staff unrest are often the results. Poor management can result in a shift in staff members' focus from their primary responsibility, teaching children, to worrying about organizational issues and daily management.

Simultaneously, when parents sense a lack of organization, they tend to become increasingly involved in questioning the management of the school. Such a lack of confidence in the administration may lead to excessive parent involvement.

As a beginning administrator, you can quickly establish yourself as an effective leader if you immediately concentrate your energies on ensuring that the school opens efficiently and effectively. If you focus on this from the moment you arrive, you will win the confidence of your constituents. This process begins with the development of positive relationships with key stakeholders.

CONNECTING WITH STAFF, PARENTS, AND STUDENTS

For most new administrators, the first test of effectiveness is what they choose to do from the moment they assume their new administrative positions. It is during these first critical weeks that others form their initial impressions of you. To a large extent, your effectiveness as an administrator will be measured by how you initially interact with teachers, support staff, parents, and students, as well as how smoothly the school year begins.

New administrators who fail to connect with constituents or mishandle staff communication or organizational tasks put themselves at a disadvantage before classes even begin. Therefore, it is important to maximize your first few weeks in your position. Here are several strategies you will want to consider.

Strategy 1: Extend an invitation to all staff to meet with you.

Staff members will be anxious about you. Some may be long tenured employees, while others may have been employed in schools where a change in the principal or assistant principal led to great staff dissatisfaction. For example, they may have had administrators who immediately identified faculty favorites, creating competition and dissension. Others may have been disorganized or unfocused, while still others may have been afraid to make a decision.

At this point, most have probably only heard about you from interview team members or met you briefly as you toured the school. Consequently, they may be nervous, especially if they were pleased with your predecessor. As a result, you must convince them that you are the type of individual who will be an effective leader.

A time-tested first step is to invite all staff members to spend a few minutes with you before the school year begins. You will want to ensure that these meetings are informal and that you make staff feel "at home." This means getting up from behind your desk and sitting with them at a conference table or in comfortable chairs. You may even want to meet with them in their classrooms rather than the office.

In addition, a comfortable room environment, free of distractions—including phone calls and interference from office personnel—and featuring well-placed refreshments, enhances the setting. Never take a phone call or respond to an e-mail or text message when you are meeting with staff. This says to them that they are not very important, which is the opposite of the message you want to send.

These sessions are most useful if you remember that the primary purpose is to get to know each other while allowing staff members to take the conversational lead. This means that they talk more and you speak less.

Good discussion starters include

- talking with them about your background and family;
- asking them about their personal experiences;

- inviting them to share what they feel proudest about in the school;
- asking them their expectations for you;
- sharing your positive impressions of the school based upon your experiences so far.

You might also want to end with a final question such as "Do you have any issues or questions about the beginning of school that I could address?" This is a good way to identify possible problem areas that you might not otherwise recognize.

These types of conversation can help you to gauge their needs as well as begin to understand the school's culture. They also help begin the relationship building process, which will be critical to your success.

Strategy 2: Invite key parents to meet with you.

In addition to staff, reaching out to parent leaders is a must. Almost every school has some type of parent-teacher organization, while some also include groups such as athletic and band boosters. If you can earn the respect of the leaders of these organizations, you will begin to solidify your reputation in the district.

Parent leaders are usually individuals with wide contact networks. Many have the ear of board members and the superintendent. If they speak positively about you, you can be assured that others will think highly of you even if they have not met you.

Along the lines of your teacher meetings, invite individuals or small groups of influential parents to have informal conversations with you. Let them get to know you on a personal level. If you have children, make sure that you discuss them, but be careful not to brag. Others may be easily turned off by this. However, parents respond well to principals and assistant principals who themselves are parents.

In these sessions, ask them what they view as the strengths of your school as well as areas in need of strengthening. Listen well and take notes. Avoid the temptation to agree to take action. A good approach is to tell them that you have high expectations for the school and value their ideas as you begin to make your initial assessment.

Strategy 3: Look for ways to involve students.

Another important group to get to know is the student body. How you do this, of course, depends to a large extent on the students' grade level. At the high school level, student leaders of school organizations can be invited to meet with you in informal, small group sessions. This is a productive way to let them know that you place a priority on student needs and will listen to what they have to say.

At both the high school and middle school levels, you should look for opportunities to invite students to assist with any number of school preparation activities. Asking faculty members to recommend students and seeking out the children of key parent leaders are effective ways to select volunteers.

These students can assist with such activities as

- freshman orientation;
- walk-in registration;
- office tasks;
- school tours for new students and their parents.

At the elementary level, there may be fewer formal options for students to be involved. Therefore, look for opportunities to meet and greet students so they feel supported and safe. Everyone expects that the principal and assistant principal will be warm, friendly, and encouraging. Parents, especially those of kindergarteners and first graders, are particularly anxious about their children's success. You can ease their fears while building relationships with their children by presenting yourself as someone who is accessible, visible, and student centered.

Always remember that if you place a priority on reaching out to staff, parents, and students during your first few weeks, the personal dividends will be substantial.

OPENING-OF-SCHOOL PLANNING

Once you have begun establishing relationships, you should turn your attention to management details. Your goal for the first day of school should be a flawless start. The reality is that this will not likely occur; but with a focus on details, you may come close to achieving it. This is a time when you must make management your number 1 priority. You can enhance your chances for success if you employ the following strategies.

Strategy 1: Focus on building on the past rather than creating the future.

One mistake novice administrators make is slipping into their role and immediately changing the way things were done in the past. They start to alter student registration and parent or teacher communication procedures without warning. You would be well served to follow past practices with minimal changes during this initial period.

Also, avoid the temptation to change too much too soon without understanding schoolwide cultural norms and the school's history. Never announce that you altered a policy or procedure to parallel the way it was in your former district!

Strategy 2: Recognize that your office staff is your institutional memory.

Often the secretary, clerk, and health aide have spent many years at the school. They know people, customs, and procedures. They can tell you if something you are considering may well lead to controversy.

They also know how "things" were done in the past and can put their hands on documents and files quickly. Insecure administrators can undermine their success by ignoring the expertise of the office staff, failing to consult with them, and trying personally to control every detail.

By seeking out your office staff's help and advice, you can increase your efficacy during your first few weeks in your position. In addition, you are actively telling office staff members that they are valued employees. By involving them, you also increase their investment in your success.

Finally, remember that inviting them into the process does not equate with empowering them to make all the decisions. As the school level administrator, you will have to decide which decisions are best to delegate and which you should keep. Through experience, you will learn best where to draw the line.

Strategy 3: Touch base with your custodial staff.

Like the office staff, your custodians have an institutional memory, in their case focused on school facilities and grounds. They can provide you with valuable insights into building operational issues and point out ways to minimize facility problems early. Too often, they feel ignored. However, by meeting with them, you also are letting them know that you know that they are important members of the school team.

Strategy 4: Ask administrative colleagues and key faculty members to review any changes in school policies and procedures before finalizing them.

If, for example, you are developing an agenda for the day that teachers return, modifying a handbook, or preparing a faculty supervision schedule, you should not do so in isolation. Rather, identify several valued individuals whom you can call for advice as well as for constructive feedback. This may very well save you from making an early critical mistake.

Strategy 5: Never send any written document to parents, school staff, or district administrators, particularly as you begin your administrative career, unless you have asked two or three individuals to edit and revise it.

As a teacher or parent yourself, you have at some point probably received a written document from an administrator littered with grammatical mistakes or poorly thought through ideas. The most effective way you can minimize these types of problems is to identify two or three individuals willing to criticize your work. It does you no good to hand a document to someone who just tells you it looks great. You have to enlist the help of individuals who are not afraid to challenge your ideas, revise your writing, and wordsmith. This means that you must insist they do so.

As a new administrator, identifying these individuals may be difficult initially. Consider asking your secretary or, if you are fortunate enough to work in a larger school, another administrator to be an editor. Support personnel such as social workers and counselors may also be options. You might even request help from another district administrator or a former colleague. You will be able to judge their helpfulness after they edit a couple of documents.

You also need to avoid the temptation to get defensive when suggestions are made, which will undermine this strategy. This approach is only effective if you are willing to accept criticism. Consider what they offer while reserving the right to make the final decision on what is written. Also, make sure that you follow this process through at least two drafts. You should ensure that you have a good dictionary and a grammar handbook, such as *The Little, Brown Compact Handbook*, by Jane E. Aaron, at your fingertips as convenient resources. Remember that you do not want to have what you wrote distributed in an educational administration graduate school class, even with identifying markers removed, as a sample of what not to do!

YOUR FIRST FACULTY MEETING

As the first day of school approaches and activity is reaching a feverish level, another key moment comes with your opening-of-school faculty meetings. For new administrators, one of the most stressful experiences is running the first faculty meeting. Whether you have fifteen or sixty teachers, you will feel as if all eyes are on you. The reality is that they are! It is good to remember that a common human reaction is to obsess about how well you will be received, which just makes you even more nervous. You will find as you gain experience that most problems you face as an administrator will not be as difficult as they appear prior to actually dealing with them.

The vast majority of teachers want you to succeed. They are probably more concerned with how you will manage the school and whether they will connect with you on a personal level. They will be worried that you will make changes with which they will be uncomfortable or that you will be difficult to work with. How you manage your first faculty meeting can diffuse much of their initial anxiety and help you get off to a good start.

To create a positive impression, consider the following strategies.

Strategy 1: Thoroughly prepare for the meeting.

One sure way to impress teachers is to be extremely well prepared and highly organized for your first meeting. This says that you are the type of leader who does his or her homework. You should review past faculty meeting agendas and touch base with office staff and key teachers to make sure you know what they are expecting. These will guide you as you prepare your agenda. Finally, ask your administrative colleagues to critique your agenda. They can offer advice on what to remove, what is missing, and any potential missteps.

Strategy 2: Create comprehensive folders with necessary documents to support your agenda.

By assembling for faculty members informational folders that contain everything needed to support your agenda, you send the message that you are highly organized. Such an approach can minimize questions while establishing a sense of organizational comfort that will ease initial teacher worries.

Strategy 3: Do not forget basic comforts.

Food, food, and more food! It is amazing how a little food and drink can make people happy. Over the years you have probably heard someone say that an easy way to make employees happy is to offer refreshments. An ample supply of pretzels and M&Ms will make staff feel physically and metaphorically comforted. By conducting your meeting in a comfortable room and providing some basic refreshments, you will set a positive tone.

Strategy 4: Keep the meeting as short as possible.

Consider for a moment how you felt as a teacher just before the first day of classes. Your primary focus was not on the strategic district goals but rather on preparing your classroom and instructional materials. This was not a time when you were thinking in terms of professional development. Novice administrators who clutter their first faculty meeting agendas with unnecessary items or use this meeting for extended discussions or professional development activities show that they are not attuned to teachers' needs. You want to let staff know that you appreciate all they have to do that first day.

Strategy 5: Be personable.

Arrive at your meeting early and try to be as calm as you can under the circumstances, even though your mind might be racing in multiple directions. If you have everything set up and ready to go beforehand, you can socialize with staff as they arrive. You will not need to think about details. Remember that a smile goes a long way!

Strategy 6: Ensure your accessibility.

During the meeting, let faculty members know where you will be available if they want to speak with you. You should try to maximize your personal availability until staff leave for the day. This means deciding to defer as much of your paperwork and management workload as possible until everyone is gone. Let unnecessary e-mails go unanswered while you focus on people. By doing this, you not only increase your personal visibility but show the staff that you see them as a priority.

Strategy 7: Takes notes on what needs to be accomplished.

Although you think you have anticipated every detail for the beginning of the school year, chances are some unanticipated issues will arise. Later in the day, some of what occurred at the meeting may seem fuzzy to you. To ensure you do not "drop any balls," you would be wise to take notes to help you remember any follow-up you may need to do.

SUMMARY

The first few weeks in your first administrative position are closely linked to your initial success. This chapter has examined what you should and should not do from the moment you assume your new position until you conclude your opening of the school year faculty meeting. Specific strategies to increase success were offered.

It's as Simple as Being Visible

*A*re you amazed at how little television and movie stars and sports figures have to do to receive adulation from the general public? If they merely appear in a public venue, it becomes an event. If they simply talk to someone or, better yet, give an autograph, they are almost deified. Later that day, that person will bubble with excitement about this chance encounter, sharing the story with friends, co-workers, and relatives. If only it were that easy to be so well liked as a school administrator!

Well, to some degree it is. You may not necessarily find yourself placed on a pedestal, but you can certainly enhance your reputation and increase your appeal through one simple action: increasing your visibility. If you make a concerted effort to be active both in and outside your school, you will no doubt discover the positive impact visibility can have. Successful school administrators understand how to build support among everyone associated with the school. They recognize the power of visibility.

Unfortunately, certain administrators create unnecessary barriers between themselves and staff. Have you ever known a principal who addressed faculty and staff members as "Mr.," "Mrs.," and "Ms.," expecting them to reciprocate with "Dr."? This level of formality interferes with an administrator's ability to establish collegial relationships.

Similarly, adopting an autocratic and nonpersonable leadership style can be alarming because it creates barriers between you and everyone else. Administrators who choose this approach seldom leave their offices, rarely visit classes, avoid hallway time, and regularly fail to greet students and parents. They often make a point of keeping their office doors closed and requiring anyone who wants to see them to make an appointment through the secretary. Needless to say, often their administrative careers in the district are relatively short.

What these individuals fail to understand is the absolute value of personal interaction and visibility. Yes, they may find administrative positions, but they may never earn the respect of teachers. These principals fail to embody what Marzano, Waters, and McNulty (2005) refer to in their twenty-one responsibilities as *visibility*, a hallmark of the most well-received and respected administrators.

As novice administrators, you will have an excellent opportunity to use personal visibility to enhance your effectiveness from your first day on the job. Discussed below are specific strategies which, if you employ them immediately, will yield positive results.

Strategy 1: Maintain an open-door policy.

Although there may be times when you cannot be available to students, staff, or parents, you will earn their respect quickly if you make visibility a priority. As a new administrator, your actions speak louder than words. From the moment you are appointed, everyone is wondering just who you really are. If you show a willingness to make yourself available without undue formality and take time to listen to anyone who wants to speak with you without appearing impatient or showing that you feel rushed (even though you may be), you will begin to model the open communication style that will help you become a successful administrator.

Strategy 2: Place a priority on school-day visibility.

Whether you are at the elementary, middle school, or high school level, one of the best ways to meet people, develop positive relations, conduct business, and stop problems before they start is to be out of your office and in the school building whenever possible. How and when this is best accomplished, of course, depends on the size and grade levels of the school you administer. By way of example, here are a few recommendations.

- Stand outside and greet students as they arrive, as well as parents dropping off children. A quick hello and smile not only lets them see you as a person but sends the message that at this school, everyone cares.
- Take a few minutes to touch base with school bus drivers during morning arrival and afternoon dismissal. You will be able to

handle some minor bus-related discipline issues before they are exacerbated. Simply assigning a student to a seat near the driver and checking in the next day to see how things went can be a simple but effective student behavior management technique. Actions such as these will build ongoing communication between you and these important support personnel who often feel "left off" the school team. In the process, you will, in all likelihood, endear yourself to those in the bus garage.

- Become a fixture in the hallways. Administrators often are quick to criticize teachers for not standing in the hallways during passing periods. However, do administrators hold themselves to the same standard? It is really easy to lose track of the bell schedule and get caught in the middle of a task or on the phone. Sometimes, of course, this is unavoidable.

  However, if you make a point of standing at the intersection of a couple of main hallways, not only can you easily reduce running and horseplay, but you can actually conduct quite a bit of business with faculty members and students. After a period of time, everyone will just know where to find you. This can actually be an effective time-management technique as well, since it reduces the "do you have a minute?" interruptions.

- Drop into the faculty lounge regularly. These visits help you connect with faculty on a personal level, as well as provide an opportunity for you to conduct school business quickly and efficiently.

- Make a point of regularly supervising, or at least dropping into, the student cafeteria. This is a good way to get to know students, lunchroom supervisors, and cafeteria personnel. It also will help you recognize potential student management issues, which you can deal with before they become more significant problems. Unstructured times such as student lunch periods can be a breeding ground for disturbances that may consume the remainder of your day.

Strategy 3: Find time to have conversations with support staff.

One key to your success is ensuring that your support staff members feel that they are respected members of the school team. Some administrators treat support personnel differently from teachers. Rather than relating to them as colleagues, they treat them as subordinates. If you want to earn the respect of the nonteaching staff, make every effort to let them know you value them and their work as much as you value the teaching faculty.

Strategy 4: Make attendance at school, district, parent-sponsored, and community functions a regular component of your personal job description.

Can you imagine conducting a screening interview for an assistant principal position during which the candidate asks about the administrator work hours? It does happen. However, you can probably also imagine how much longer that interview continued. You have to remember that building-level administrators are closely associated with the school. In essence, how you are perceived by constituents is often translated into overall public perception of the school. An excellent strategy for improving your school's image is the simple practice of taking time to attend as many functions as reasonable.

As an administrator, you must recognize the importance of "being seen" at multiple functions and school activities. In most instances, your actual responsibilities will be quite minimal. You will usually be expected to socialize with students, employees, parents, and community members. Although these events will add significantly to your working hours, they will also help you sense the "pulse" of your stakeholders while building positive relationships. The more others see you as an approachable, friendly, enthusiastic leader, the more support you will build, not only for your school but for yourself.

Strategy 5: Become a fixture at school board meetings.

As a new administrator, you will discover that some superintendents require building administrators to attend school board meetings, while others do not. What you always want to remember is that the board of education is your ultimate boss. Yes, board members typically defer to the superintendent regarding administrative performance; but in reality, they are responsible for awarding your employment contract and approving your annual salary. In many districts, principals' salary increases are influenced by their working relationships with board members.

If you think about it, most of the information board members receive about you comes through central office administrators, parents, and teachers. By attending school board meetings, where you will periodically make presentations; where you will be available to answer questions; and where you will socialize with board members, you will ensure that they get to know you on both a personal and professional level, rather than relying almost exclusively on others' comments.

In some districts, administrators' contracts and salaries are presumably merit based. However, in reality, "merit" is often based on your reputation in the district. If both parents and teachers let board members know that they are happy with you, your reputation with the board of education will be enhanced. As a consequence, your salary increase may very well be influenced by this informal "merit" system.

Administrators who regularly attend school board meetings build strong relationships with board members, while softening the impact of less than positive parent and staff comments. As a new administrator, you will want to maximize your visibility at board meetings even if attendance is voluntary.

Strategy 6: Make instructional supervision a daily priority.

It is very easy for building administrators to find themselves glued to their offices. The array of never-ending e-mails, phone calls, management tasks, and problem solving can consume you. Some principals become so busy with these types of activities that they place instructional supervision to the side. They are so "office anchored" that when they walk into a classroom, a student might ask the teacher, "Who is this?" In other instances, where principals are highly visible, when they enter classrooms students immediately beam with approval and try to catch the principals' attention.

Classroom visibility not only enhances a building administrator's relationship with students but also pays dividends with parents. When children come home and discuss their day, especially at the elementary level, they will invariably mention the principal's visit. Since parents closely align their perceptions of the school with the success and happiness of their children, any positive attention by the principal is well received.

In addition, classroom visibility is important for instructional leadership. Some administrators follow principals who served for decades and with whom the faculty members were very comfortable. These veteran teachers may have become used to a laissez-faire approach to supervision, under which they were rarely observed by the principal in their classrooms. In essence, they were permitted to do whatever they chose to do. Unfortunately, these types of schools often earn a reputation as status quo oriented or the "weak stepsister" of the district.

If you are a visible administrator, what you will discover as a new principal is that you may be greeted with skepticism. At first, teachers may be uncomfortable with you. Some may be very nervous when you drop into their rooms. You may even be reminded that the former principal never did this. However, the most successful administrators recognize that visibility is crucial to their success and continue being very active throughout the school.

To respond to such situations, an effective approach is to look for reasons to drop into classrooms. Consider such strategies as personally delivering the school's daily bulletin and personal messages to classrooms. In general, look for grade-level appropriate opportunities to assert your visibility. What you will discover after a period of time is that your regular visits will soon be accepted. In fact, do not be surprised if teachers look forward to your drop-in visits.

Once your visibility is well established, you will be better positioned not only to build relationships with teachers and students but also to begin to focus on instructional improvement. Successful building administrators look for such opportunities and use them to their advantage.

You can begin to build visibility while enhancing your supervision and instructional-leadership skills through some simple yet effective techniques. However, before implementing any of these, make sure that you have the authority to do so under your school district's collective bargaining agreement.

Daily Walk-through Visits

One highly effective way to increase your visibility is to conduct what are termed *daily walk-through visits*. As noted earlier, administrators are busy people. If they do not consciously set aside some time each school day for classroom visits, the reality is that they will seldom get to them. An approach that works well is to make a commitment to set aside some time for daily classroom visits. Often these visits last only a minute or two, but they are nonetheless well received by teachers who want to know that the principal cares about what they are doing.

It is important to remember that most faculty members want some attention and welcome feedback from the school level administrators. However, principals of very large schools may have to spread their visits our over two or more days. By building walk-through visits into your schedule, you may not only increase your general visibility with students and staff, but also develop a feel for what is being taught throughout the building.

Classroom Walk-throughs

There is no one classroom walk-through model. In fact, walk-through approaches may include teachers, educators from other school districts, and even parents, in addition to the building school administrators. Kachur, Stout, and Edwards (2010), in their book *Classroom Walkthroughs to Improve Teaching and Learning*, discuss eighteen different walk-through approaches employed throughout the United States. Most are specifically designed for use by building administrators.

Mini-Observations

Marshall (2009) describes another approach, which she has termed the *mini-observation*. In addition to walk-through visits and formal teacher observations that are required as part of your district's teacher evaluation process, another effective instructional leadership approach is to build five mini-observations of up to fifteen minutes each into your daily schedule.

You will discover, as most experienced administrators have, that you can gather a great deal of information about a teacher's performance in a relatively short period of time. Although you may not always be able to complete all your mini-observations each day, by setting this as a goal for yourself, you will increase your presence in classrooms.

To help focus your mini-observations, Marshall (2009) suggests that you concentrate on several specific areas. You will want to ask yourself the following questions as you visit classrooms:

- Are there any physical safety concerns?
- Is the classroom environment psychologically safe?
- What is the lesson objective?
- How effective is the teacher's instruction?
- Are students engaged and active in the learning process?
- Is there evidence of student assessment?

Since your visit is relatively brief, you will not see evidence in all these areas, but you will probably leave with perceptions in at least two areas.

One difference between mini-observations and daily walk-through observations is feedback to the teacher. Rather than formalizing this process, which can be very time-consuming, you will want to look for opportunities to share informal feedback following a mini-observation. Marshall (2009) suggests a brief conversation in the hallway, at lunch, or during a planning period. Remember that the best feedback is specific to the teacher you observed. Merely telling the teacher that everything was wonderful is essentially useless. Remember how you reacted when an administrator provided global, nonpersonalized, overly positive compliments?

By the way, you must ensure that mini-observations do not become associated with the formal evaluation process, or you will defeat their purpose. These should be viewed as formative supervision designed to foster professional growth, not a vehicle to make summative judgments about a teacher's performance.

Informal Classroom Observations

Zepeda (2007) also discusses the importance of informal observations, not only for visibility but as a means of reinforcing what teachers are doing well. She notes that the advantages of informal observations include motivating teachers, assessing instruction, increasing your accessibility, and providing teachers with support. In addition, she points out that this strategy helps the administrator stay informed about classroom instruction (Blase and Blase, 1998).

By utilizing each of these approaches, you will show that you are placing a high priority on instructional supervision. At the same time, you will be building positive, collegial relationships with faculty members.

SUMMARY

Administrative visibility is critical to getting off to a good start as an administrator. Those who place a high value on visibility recognize that it is a tool which they can use to conduct school business, demonstrate a commitment to professional growth, and enhance professional and personal relationships. As a new administrator, you should never miss an opportunity to use visibility to enhance your professional reputation.

· 4 ·

Building Relationships within the School

$\mathcal{A}$bsolutely critical to any administrator's success is the ability to develop positive relationships. At times, even some experienced administrators sabotage their careers by what they do or fail to do. Even superintendents can damage their effectiveness relatively quickly if they fail to use relationship-building strategies when managing significant school district problems.

One stumbling block that interferes with relationship building is limited perspective. You will want to remember that teachers and parents do not have as broad a perspective on issues as administrators. This is a significant issue that you will face as a new administrator. In fact, the narrowness of employee and parent perspectives can be a source of frustration for administrators.

First-time administrators are sometimes naive enough to believe that all they have to do when they make a decision is explain their rationale. They assume that because they have been teachers, surely staff will understand and support their decisions because they are looking out for everyone's best interests.

What they quickly learn, though, is that not everyone agrees with them, and that sometimes there are nearly as many different positions on issues as there are people involved. In fact, for the first time in his or her career, an administrator may find him- or herself being treated as an outsider, not as one of the faculty. The administrator knows that he or she has not changed as a person in the past few months, but others have altered their perceptions. Just because they are now administrators, these individuals are perceived as somewhat less trustworthy.

One of the first hurdles you must clear as a novice administrator is accepting the reality that you are no longer a member of the teaching faculty and that your relationships with staff will be different. To a large extent, your relationships will be more professional than personal. This change can be especially significant if you assume an administrative position within the same school in which you taught. Once you recognize and accept this change, you will be ready to move forward as an administrator, and you'll be prepared to build professional relationships—which Marzano, Waters, and McNulty (2005) point out is important for successful school leadership.

Beginning administrators can make critical relationship mistakes during their first few months. One of the first is failing to recognize the necessity of treating all staff members similarly. Often a new administrator is naturally attracted to positive, supportive employees rather than those who are less social or more critical. In their excitement to emphasize the positive, these principals develop visible alliances with certain teachers.

Since these staff members are usually friendlier and outwardly supportive, the tendency is to spend more public time with them, even socializing outside of school. Unfortunately, by doing so, new administrators create "camps of favorites," which sends the message to some staff that they are not as highly valued.

One way new administrators undermine their success is by unwittingly incorporating certain information in their weekly staff bulletins. In their enthusiasm to be viewed as positive leaders, they include a section in which they recognize individual staff member accomplishments. If, for example, the music teachers conduct a successful school concert, they are congratulated in the weekly bulletin. What novice principals fail to recognize is that by singling out certain teachers for public recognition, they may inadvertently damage teacher morale and create dissatisfaction among others.

Similarly, when you become an administrator, be cognizant of the fact that teachers watch what relationships principals develop with staff members. They want to see whether you align with one staff group over another. This may be as simple as watching whom you choose to sit with during the staff holiday party or even lunch periods. The more you can maintain a relatively equal professional relationship with staff, the more easily you can avoid the pitfalls of playing favorites.

As you begin your administrative career, you can avoid many novice missteps by applying several strategies.

Strategy 1: Place a priority on learning about the school's unspoken culture.

A mistake beginning administrators make is assuming that school culture and accompanying norms are very similar from one school to another. The reality is that while one issue may generate a flurry of faculty comment in one school, it is not even on the radar screen in another. In some schools, such tasks as developing parent-conference procedures and selecting dates and times can lead to controversy, while in others, gum chewing is a hot topic. What is an issue in one school may not be in another. If you want to avoid being labeled an authoritarian leader, consider bouncing ideas off at least some key faculty members before you make any quick or wide-ranging decisions.

Strategy 2: Try to maintain balanced relationships with all faculty members. Avoid excessive public praising.

At one time or another, you probably attended a class in which the teacher played favorites. Assuming you were not the favorite, think about how you felt at the time. As a novice administrator, it is in your best interest to make every effort to treat staff equitably. At the same time, you will find certain faculty members whose opinions you value and who share similar views about children and the direction of the school. You will want to ensure that you show them that you value their opinions and support, but in a nonpublic way.

Strategy 3: Take time to get to know your staff members on a personal level.

Some administrators never want to be too close with any staff members because at some point they worry that they may have to discipline or even terminate one of them. Often what these administrators have in common is that they are outwardly personable but difficult to get to know beyond a superficial level.

School leaders who avoid such artificial personal barriers can actually have a greater impact in their schools because the relationships they establish are perceived as more genuine. Yes, as an administrator, at times you may have to deal with uncomfortable situations and still have to make difficult decisions; but by connecting personally with staff, you also will enhance your chances for creating a collaborative school culture.

As beginning administrators, you can start to create positive, productive relationships with your staff by

- making time to join them during lunch on a regular basis;
- dropping into classrooms and office areas just to chat;
- showing an interest in them as individuals;
- reaching out to faculty members who may have problems or special needs, which might mean permitting them some flexibility to arrive late or leave early under certain circumstances;
- practicing good listening;

- sharing information openly about yourself and your family, but ensuring that you do not become too personal by sharing information such as weekend partying or personal habits;
- encouraging faculty members to initiate social events;
- participating in as many staff, school, and district-sponsored events as feasible.

Strategy 4: Assess relationships between staff members.

As a new administrator, you will want to study interpersonal relationships among staff members. What you will discover is that some staff members work well together, while others do not. These relationships can either enhance or inhibit how well the school functions. To assess faculty relationships, watch who tends to spend time with whom, whom people choose to sit with in formal and informal settings, and how people interact during meetings. By studying how staff members relate, you will gain information that you can use to increase your effectiveness as the leader.

Strategy 5: Treat all employees with respect.

As with any employee group, you have some individuals who are exceptionally dedicated and competent. For example, you may have a custodian who takes great pride in everything he or she does. Day in and day out, your classroom is always immaculate. The custodian may also have an engaging personality, and, as a consequence, you may have quickly learned a great deal about the custodian and his or her family. For these individuals, in particular, relationship building and being treated with respect by administrators are very important.

A small percentage of administrators make the mistake of ignoring nonteaching staff members and treating them more like low-valued employees than colleagues. It is important for you to recognize the inherent dignity in everyone. Just because someone has a higher level of education or more decision making authority, or earns a higher salary, this does not mean that the person is better than someone else.

As a beginning administrator, you can enhance your personal success by demonstrating respect for all employees no matter whether they are teachers, bus drivers, custodians, clerical staff, or teaching assistants. Avoid the temptation to focus your energies primarily on the faculty and other administrators. Rather, show support staff that they are respected and valued. You might be surprised how a few positive comments from a support staff member can affect others' perceptions of you.

Although it is important to build positive relations with all support personnel, no one is more important to your success than the school secretary. Remember that the school secretary is frequently a member of the local school community, while at the same time privy to confidential information. Secretaries take great pride in the knowledge they have and enjoy offering their expertise to their building administrators. For all practical purposes, they are often the institutional memory of the school. As such, they can be an invaluable source of information and also help you avoid a myriad of management and political traps. At the same time, though, a few well-placed comments from the secretary can scuttle your success.

In order to build a solid working relationship with your secretary, you will want to recognize that a key to making this relationship most effective is letting office staff know your expectations and priorities. Have you ever stopped by a school office as a parent or visitor and found yourself ignored or treated with disrespect by the person greeting you? If so, remember how you felt.

As an administrator, you have great influence over the image and service level of the school office. A negative experience by a visitor or another school employee will reflect poorly on you. Therefore, an important first step when you assume your first administrative position is to articulate your expectations to the office staff who greet visitors.

Equally important is learning to delegate. Inefficient and sometimes insecure novice administrators feel they need to be involved in everything, including all decision making. To enhance your effectiveness, identify what you can delegate to your secretary, then give the person the authority to respond. Rather than sending an "I don't trust you" message, you will empower your office staff and free up valuable time for yourself to manage the complex tasks of building-level leadership.

Strategy 6: Avoid the temptation to make too many changes too quickly.

One common experience many administrators share is what I call "getting your marching orders." They typically come from your superintendent if you are a principal, or from your principal if you are an assistant principal. At some point, either just before you actually assume your position or shortly thereafter, you may meet with your supervisor, who will discuss with you various issues and problems that you are expected to address during your first year or two.

Often superintendents give their assessment of the strengths and weaknesses of the school and identify what areas they expect you to improve. The message is loud and clear. Principals, too, have similar conversations with new assistant principals, although the tone may be less demanding and more collaborative—but nonetheless direct.

When new administrators are hired, they are never told to maintain the status quo. Supervisors and boards of education typically view changes in leadership as opportunities to improve the school. As you go through the administrative interview process, you should be able to detect what these priorities might be.

To a large extent, your success as an administrator will be judged on how well you address these "agenda" items. However, no matter how time sensitive many of them appear, you would be wise to keep your pace slower rather than faster your first year. This is an especially critical period for any new administrator since this is when most stakeholders form their impressions of you. One way to alienate almost everyone is to come in and start to make changes from day 1. If you really want to submarine your success, just begin your comments with such statements as "This is how we did it at my former school."

Rather, a better approach is to take some time to observe all aspects of the school and listen to those who work for you and those for whom you work. Remember, most people neither expect nor want immediate change. Spend some time exploring what the faculty expects of you. If you move too quickly, you run the risk of being viewed as an autocrat and a poor team player. Think for a moment. How can you ask faculty members to be collaborative if you impose dramatic changes without inviting collaboration?

Strategy 7: Consider forming a faculty leadership team.

A sound strategy to involve faculty members appropriately while simultaneously hearing what is on their minds is to create a school leadership team. By inviting representatives of various grade levels and content areas to meet with you on a regular basis, you develop a clearer sense of faculty perceptions while improving internal communication. To avoid a "complaint committee," be sure to communicate clearly the purposes, goals, and procedures of the committee as you initiate the process.

Strategy 8: Make students a priority.

No matter what level of school you administer, if you make students a priority, you will enhance your relationships with everyone. Beyond adult relationships, those established with students are crucial to your success. Remember that schools are all about children; however, some assistant principals and even principals take pride in being stern authoritarians who are almost consumed with discipline. Their actions espouse the "never smile until spring break" philosophy. Taking such an approach is a sure way to alienate not only students but parents and most teachers.

Even though the way administrators relate with students varies depending upon the level of school they administer, the principles behind their actions are the same. Administrators who take a true interest in students and seek ways to interact with them bolster their positive reputations within the school and general community. This means making student interactions a planned part of your day.

Some elementary principals develop enormously positive reputations. Not only are they visible instructional leaders, but they have a unique ability to connect with children through special activities. One simple way to reinforce the value of reading and also connect with students is to develop reading-related activities. One approach might be to draw the name of one student weekly, for whom you buy a book—which you personally deliver to the student's home. Once there, you read a portion of the book and take time to visit with the family. Such proactive, visible events can create quite a buzz with both students and parents.

Sporting activities also allow building-level administrators to connect with students, while increasing the productivity of recess and lunch time. Elementary principals who make a point of regularly dropping in to recess, where they organize pickup basketball and volleyball games that include both boys and girls, can quickly connect with students. If you are especially clever, you can alter the game rules to fit the age level of the students, always making sure that each student has the opportunity to participate. This might even include serving as the team's captain, making sure to pass the ball to all and encouraging everyone to shoot.

Not only would this simple approach build positive relationships with students, but it would help focus students on productive activities during minimally structured times when they might otherwise get into some mischief.

Middle school principals and assistants can also organize basketball and softball games, as well as free-throw shooting contests, as part of lunch activities. Students really enjoy seeing if they can sink more free throws in ten tries than the assistant principal. You can endear yourself even further by giving a coupon for a free cafeteria ice cream to anyone who can shoot more free throws out of ten than you.

Although the last two examples are sports related, any other type of student-focused activity would have a parallel effect. For example, principals can create a weekly student birthday recognition luncheon for all students who had birthdays that week. You can even set aside time for those with birthdays during vacation periods.

This same principle of positive interaction with students is equally applicable at the high school. High school administrators who mingle in the hallways with students by striking up conversations and showing both interest and enthusiasm can quickly establish positive relationships. You can make a point of getting to know as much about various students' school involvement activities as possible, and use passing periods and lunch times to create conversations with groups of students around the information you have gathered.

What makes these tactics special is that you do not focus only on sports successes but rather on personal student accomplishments, all while taking the time to get to know other students as well. Too often, particularly at the high school level, administrators become office-bound and adult focused.

Each of these ideas seems rather self-evident, but each is often forgotten in the "busyness" of the school day. As a new administrator, you will find that having these types of personal interactions with students can yield extraordinary dividends not only with students but also with parents and staff. You will also want to remember that many parents judge the quality of the school through their children's experiences. Therefore, when their children are happy and successful, parents' perceptions of you as well as the school in general are enhanced.

Strategy 9: Win over the parent–teacher organization.

As a building-level administrator, you need to recognize that the parent-teacher organization (PTO) is vital to your success. Did you ever sit in a graduate school class during your administrative leadership program and listen to other students, or even guest speakers, describing how difficult it was to work with their parent-teacher organizations? You have probably heard of principals who were "run out of their positions" by their parent organizations.

Monthly PTO meetings can become contentious, with parent factions arguing over various agenda items, sometimes until late into the evening. In some schools, the situation can deteriorate to the point that certain parents begin micromanaging aspects of the school through the school secretary and individual teachers. Principals who have this level of discord often lose their positions.

Although dysfunctional parent organizations can develop even under the leadership of an effective principal, more often than not, building-level administrators can develop a good working relationship with their parent groups if they understand certain principles. Below are suggestions you may want to consider.

Learn how your PTO board is organized and what their expectations are for you.

Many novice administrators who deal with the parent organization for the first time are unfamiliar with their role relative to the organization. As teachers, they may never have attended a parent board meeting, or, if they did, they may have just observed a portion of the meeting without ever understanding the format. Thus, without some counsel from a successful principal or some background learning as part of the administrative preparation program, the new administrator may be at a significant disadvantage upon walking into that first PTO meeting.

What you can expect is that parent boards are generally organized around a committee structure that reflects what the organization plans to accomplish during the year. You can be assured that there will be some sort of fund-raising committee, whether the activities consist of an elaborate series of fund-raising events throughout the year, or simple fund-generating tasks such as selling school spirit sweat suits and T-shirts, collecting money from the photographers as part of student picture day, or selling gym suits.

In addition, special school events supported by the PTO, such as a graduation party, a cultural arts program, or a needy family support fund, usually require a committee. As a result of this committee process, each board meeting is composed primarily of reports from subcommittees.

In schools, parent volunteers serve two distinct purposes: they provide both labor and monetary support. If their efforts are channeled properly, parent boards can provide valuable school support.

As a new administrator, you will need to recognize that for these parents, whatever they contribute, no matter how small, is very important to them. In essence, they are helping their children. You need to exercise great patience sometimes during long meetings spent listening intently to committee reports. You would be well served to learn how to offer encouragement and support even if you know that what they are discussing could much more easily and effectively be provided by the school staff. These parents want to feel a part of the school community and can be your biggest supporters if they like and respect you. They can be real trouble if they do not.

Be prepared to present a principal's report at the beginning of each PTO board meeting.

As part of every parent board meeting, expect to make a principal's report. This is actually a great opportunity to win the approval of the parents. The best way to approach these reports is to remember two things: parents are there for their children, and they expect that good things are happening at the school. With these things in mind, you will want to make sure that during your report you focus on children first. Anything you can offer about what is happening in school for their children, or even what is planned for the year, will be well received.

Successful principals devise creative ways to promote both the school and the students. One good approach is to develop a schoolwide slideshow through which you can showcase your school and, at the same time, send the message that your school is a happy and productive place.

A way to accomplish this is to invite two students to serve as school photographers. During the year, make a point of escorting them around the school during the day, as well as before and after school, to take as many photographs as possible. As part of this process, make sure that they have not missed any staff member and that they capture as many events as is realistic. Go to great lengths to ensure that those photographed are engaged in productive activities and, if at all possible, that they are smiling and happy. After the photography portion is completed, work with the students to select some up-tempo music and prepare an automatic slideshow.

Your student-prepared show is now ready for presentation at the parent board meeting, new student orientation programs, and any other events in which you plan to showcase your school. If you invite your student photographers to present their show, you will only enhance its marketing power. Needless to say, you can probably imagine what a hit special activities such as this are.

In addition to such special student-related activities, you should make a point of using the principal's report time to highlight the school goals, new programs, and various services. Parents expect your school to be continuously improving. For most, this means that the educational program is improving and that, as principal, you are looking for ways to build upon what exists. By highlighting the academic and special programs, you not only show your accomplishments but send the message that this is a school that is growing. Administrators who fail to do so run the risk of being perceived by parents as "status quo" oriented and may create the impression that the school is living on its past laurels.

Strategy 10: Recognize that less is more.

One potentially fatal tendency of new administrators is overcommunication. The key is maintaining a balance of communication. Time and time again, administrators operate on the premise that the more information they share with others and the more they involve others in decision making, the greater their likelihood of success. Unless you are a master communicator, you are probably actually reducing your chances for success and inviting micromanagement.

The reality is that administrators would be well served if they lived by the motto "less is more." You need to remind yourself continuously that once you start a new program or invite others into the decision-making process, the more you will hear, "What have you done for me lately?" Think about it for a moment: if you inaugurate a biweekly principal's bulletin for parents with no express purpose other than to convince them that you are a strong communicator, how long will it be before they want it every week? The tendency of constituents is to always want more, never a reduction in what is offered.

This is where less is actually more. You can increase your effectiveness and maintain good support if you ensure that whenever you increase communication or invite others to participate in decision making, you have a sound reason for doing so. Otherwise, you invite micromanagement and potential distress.

As the school leader, you control the substance and flow of information to the parent organizations. What you need to recognize is that you must decide what it is that you want them to hear and on what topics you want their opinions. However, if there is an "elephant in the room," you should not ignore it. Your goal is to find the appropriate level of communication where they feel "in the loop." Novice administrators would be wise to minimize the information they provide to their staff and parent boards until they understand not only how to work effectively with various groups, but also what information will contribute to productive relationships.

Sometimes beginning administrators try too hard to impress their parent organizations by making them privy to too much information. You might think it is a good idea to discuss some minor bullying issues at an open parent-board meeting and solicit their advice on how to best handle these cases. You might think that by sharing what is happening in the school and asking parent opinions, you will be viewed as a proactive leader. Unfortunately, this simple conversation can explode into a flurry of unintended consequences.

Parents may go home and ask their children about bullying, with the result that they return to school shaken. Just asking the question may exacerbate the level of responses. Negative teachers may see this as an opportunity to complain to parents about a lack of discipline and poor administrative support. The local newspaper may write a story about the school's bullying problems after being contacted by a school parent. Before long, a simple gesture designed to involve the parent board can became an all-consuming schoolwide issue.

This story illustrates how quickly a beginning administrator can create unnecessary and unwanted problems without realizing it. As a new administrator, you will want to seek the advice of experienced administrators who have been successful and who can help you think through your actions and recognize when less really is more.

SUMMARY

Probably nothing is more important than building positive relationships with the school community. In this chapter, we have examined strategies beginning administrators can use to work most effectively with key stakeholders. Remember that building positive relations is one of the keys to a new administrator's success.

Working with Other Administrators

$\mathcal{A}$s a teacher, you are automatically a member of a large group of colleagues who interact with each other daily from the moment they walk into the faculty lounge in the morning until they leave at the end of the day. These interactions may be personal or purely social, but they are also professional. When a teacher has a problem, often all the teacher has to do is turn to a colleague in the next classroom.

One of the adjustments you will discover as an administrator is that your support base may be initially nonexistent, especially if you are the only administrator in your building. Because of this reality, most administrators reach out to their district colleagues or administrators in other school districts. Yet even with this network, you will feel some sense of isolation.

Since administrative collegial relationships are important to any administrator's success, an understanding of how to relate to everyone from the superintendent to other district administrators to colleagues in other school districts can enhance your personal success.

SUPERINTENDENT RELATIONS

For the most part, superintendents understand the value of collegial relationships. Most began as building administrators and experienced the transition from teaching to administration. However, as they advanced in their careers, their professional focus likely shifted from the building to the district level. As superintendents, they are responsible for the overall management of the district and issues related primarily to adults, not children.

Because superintendents are stretched very thin, the time they have available to mentor new administrators is limited. Also, since their success is often linked to the efficiency and effectiveness of the district, they tend to focus primarily on the board of education, parents, and employees. Consequently, you should expect to have a cordial and professional, rather than personal, relationship with your superintendent.

Superintendents generally do not expect to be enmeshed too frequently in specific school-related problems, but they also know that problems are endemic to leadership. For the most part, they want their school administrators to manage school-based problems whenever possible without their direct involvement. However, in smaller school districts, the superintendent may be more directly involved in school-based operational issues. In these circumstances, you will find yourself problem solving directly with your superintendent, much as you would with other administrative colleagues.

While superintendents want building-level administrators to handle school issues, a key to maintaining a good working relationship with your superintendent is communication. You want to remember that boards of education and superintendents do not like surprises. One sure way to undermine your success is to fail to keep your superintendent informed about problems and issues. Both superintendents and board members will, in all likelihood, hear about issues whether you tell them or not. This may occur at the supermarket, a school event, or a cocktail party, or during a call to the superintendent's or board member's home.

You never want to be in a position where the first time your superintendent learns about something controversial is at a school board meeting, from a disgruntled parent, employee, or board member. As a new administrator, you want to inform your superintendent first about anything you anticipate may "float up" to the central office or school board level.

At the same time, you must also exercise caution not to overinform. As noted earlier, superintendents are extremely busy. They hire building administrators because they believe that they have the management and leadership skills to administer their schools or specific program areas efficiently. New administrators who overinform or seek advice too frequently on issues they are expected to resolve in their schools can weaken their relationships with their superintendents.

Consequently, after you assume your first administrative position, you will need to decide what information should be shared and what should not. An effective strategy to help you make these decisions is to use administrators both within and outside your school district as sounding boards.

Superintendents also expect their administrators to be team players who recognize their allegiances to the administrative team. One mistake novice administrators make is thinking that they can maintain the same level of collegiality with school employees that they had as teachers. They assume that teachers will understand the difficult decisions they have to make and are surprised when they are questioned or not supported by teachers. Once you recognize that you are an administrator and not a teacher, you can become more effective.

Certain inexperienced administrators try to avoid their administrative team responsibilities. When decisions are made at the district level that are either controversial or unpopular, especially with teachers, some principals tell faculty members that these decisions were not theirs but rather "came down" from the central office. This is particularly common when principals need to reduce budget allocations or cut staff. Administrators who take this approach think that they are solidifying their faculty support. But, in reality, they are sending the message that they are not the "real" school leaders.

Employees understand, although they may never say it, that administrators periodically have to make unpopular decisions. Even though they may initially express disapproval, in the long run they will respect administrators who are straightforward and willing to take responsibility for their decisions. If they sense that you are not the decision maker, before long they will begin to bypass you and go directly to central office administrators.

Trying to appease employees also can undermine your reputation with the superintendent and other central office administrators. Consider how you might react if you were the superintendent, and you discovered that your principals let teachers believe that they did not support your decisions but were required to enforce them.

Another way in which inexperienced administrators can damage their relationships with superintendents is through a lack of conviction. It is natural when you assume a beginning administrative position to want to earn the respect of central office administrators, especially the superintendent. However, *pleasing* is not a synonym for *earning*. A new administrator should not try to read the superintendent's position and take that position regardless of his or her own feelings on the issue. Rather, superintendents want administrative team members who are willing to state their opinions as part of an open exchange of ideas yet who are flexible enough to be collaborative in the decision-making process.

Key to this collaboration is a team, as opposed to competitive, personal orientation. Although a small number of superintendents prefer to build a competitive administrative environment, most want to assemble an administrative team that solves problems together. Unlike in competitive environments, in which individual administrators try to "outshine" their colleagues, those on collaborative teams are expected to understand that the success of the group outweighs personal interests. As team members, they are expected to assist each other in making good decisions.

To demonstrate collaborative team skills, you will want to

- be a good listener and not overtalk;
- express your point of view in the spirit of the best decision for the team;
- be willing to point out any potential positive as well as negative consequences of a topic under discussion that the team needs to consider;
- base your assessment of others' ideas on merit rather than your relationships with them;
- commit to compromise, not to winning;
- show support for your colleagues;
- present your ideas and opinions in a calm, thoughtful, nonaggressive manner.

A good test of whether you might be perceived by others as a team player is to ask yourself whether you would want yourself on the team if you were the superintendent. District leaders know that a solid administrative team generally makes more informed decisions, and minimizes the poor decisions that are more likely when a single administrator is the sole decision maker.

Team skills are not genetic, but rather learned. A good time to practice developing your team-orientation skills is when you are a teacher. Your success in this area will not only allow you to grow as an individual but also show your present administrator, who may either hire you for an administrative position or be one of your references, that you have the skills necessary for successful leadership.

THE SUPERVISOR/SUPERVISEE RELATIONSHIP

No matter how well you work with your superintendent, the reality is that the superintendent is your supervisor. As a beginning administrator, you need to understand what the superintendent expects of you. Some will be very direct. Even during the interview process, they will tell you what needs to be accomplished. After you are officially employed, they may even ask you to develop specific personal and/or school goals related to their expectations.

In other instances, superintendents may have certain expectations but never discuss them with you. This can be problematic, particularly if your performance evaluation or even your salary increase will be partially based on your perceived performance in these areas.

Unlike teacher evaluation processes, which are linked to collective bargaining agreements and state laws, administrative evaluation requirements are traditionally left to the discretion of the superintendent and school board. As a result, administrative evaluation procedures vary greatly from school district to school district. In some, they may not even exist or be so informal that they appear meaningless. However, some states, such as Illinois, have mandated principal evaluation standards.

On the other hand, you do not want to mistake a lack of structure or formality for job security or a sign that your performance is acceptable. You may be unpleasantly surprised later in the year, when your contract is up for renewal.

Since administrative evaluation procedures can appear elusive, superintendents may or may not directly state their expectations for administrators. As a result, it may be necessary for you to take the initiative to understand how your superintendent evaluates administrators in your district. Several possible strategies that you could employ are discussed below.

Strategy 1: Ask other administrators how they were evaluated.

Since they have been through the process, they can tell you how "it really works." You will be able to gather information not readily available from others, or more details on how any written procedures actually work. As you have these conversations, you will want to be as confidential as possible. You never want to share what one administrator told you with another. Also, since each administrator may have had a different relationship with the superintendent, their individual perceptions may vary. By meeting with more than one administrative colleague, you can weigh what you have discovered before drawing any definitive conclusions.

Strategy 2: Meet with other central office administrators to gather their perceptions on the administrative evaluation process and what is expected of you.

Although central office administrators, because they are typically part of the superintendent's team, may not be quite as frank as building-level colleagues about your district's administrative evaluation process, they can provide additional insights. They may be especially useful in helping you understand what the superintendent expects from you.

Strategy 3: Make an appointment with the superintendent to discuss priorities and goals.

During the meeting, it is important to let the superintendent know that you are committed to being a highly effective administrator and would value any insights or suggestions. Your openness may be the catalyst needed for a productive conversation, especially with superintendents who might otherwise not discuss their expectations for you.

RELATIONSHIPS WITH CENTRAL OFFICE ADMINISTRATORS

If you have the good fortune to work in a school district large enough to have a central office administrative staff, you will find that they can be an excellent resource. They can guide you through district policies and procedures while giving you a "heads-up" on potential issues. However, you also must understand how to work effectively with them.

It is critical to recognize their responsibilities as well as what they expect of you. District-level administrators such as assistant superintendents or coordinators for instruction, special services, or business have very specific responsibilities and must report their progress to the superintendent and board of education on a regular basis. Since they are not principals with direct authority over a substantial staff, they rely on principals and assistant principals not only for information but also for assistance.

You can enhance your working relationship with central office administrators by

- asking them what you could do to assist them;
- meeting their deadlines;
- ensuring that reports and forms are completed thoroughly and accurately;
- volunteering to serve with them on district committees;
- taking the initiative on activities, projects, supervision, and communications related to your school that fall within their scope of responsibilities;
- supporting their efforts with your faculty and staff members;
- avoiding overcommunicating with them over unnecessary items that you could manage on your own;
- keeping them in the "loop" on issues in your building that relate to their areas of responsibility before they become a problem.

You should remember that a central office administrator can be your "best friend," especially when you need help resolving problems, working with the superintendent, or communicating with the board. If they are supportive of you, they may look out for you. Principals who have positive working relationships with their business managers will tell you how the business manager anticipated a particular financial issue and resolved it before it was even noticed.

RELATIONSHIPS WITH OTHER DISTRICT ADMINISTRATORS

As discussed earlier, administration can be lonely. You can have a professional relationship with your superintendent and other central office administrators, but often you must turn to other colleagues for more personal relationships.

On the other hand, your relationships with other principals or assistant principals are more likely to be collegial, since you each share common concerns and similar responsibilities without the supervisory connection. However, establishing positive collegial administrative relationships can be complicated.

Even though your natural tendency may be to seek out personal and professional relationships with building-level colleagues, you will discover that not all administrators share this goal. Some believe that their success is linked to your failure, especially if they work in a school district where the superintendent values competition rather than cooperation. The use of merit pay administrative compensation models often exacerbates an already competitive environment.

On the other hand, you will also find other administrators who value cooperation as a vehicle for professional support. For them, the value of having an administrative colleague whom they can trust to maintain confidentiality when discussing school-related issues, and to whom they can turn for unqualified support and advice, is immeasurable.

Finally, as a novice administrator, you will want to move slowly as you attempt to "fit in" with your colleagues. You would be well served to spend some time watching how administrative team members interact and assessing their openness to collegiality. This will permit you to gauge their commitment to collaboration while also allowing them to get to know you.

To build positive administrative collegial relationships, consider using the following strategies.

Strategy 1: Maintain a "half-full" rather than "half-empty" perspective.

How do you normally react to people who are always complaining or criticizing others? Most individuals tend to avoid the chronic complainers if at all possible. These types of administrators are usually fault-finders. They take pleasure in saying why something will not work rather than offering constructive suggestions. On the other hand, individuals who stress the positive, display a sense of humor, and show enthusiasm tend to attract others.

Strategy 2: Avoid the "know-it-all" syndrome.

One sure way to alienate your administrative colleagues and others as well is to be a "know-it-all." These individuals typically have either below-average self-perception skills or are very insecure. Commonly, they display two particular characteristics. First, they portray themselves as knowing more than everyone else in the group, even if they have limited experiences. If you share a problem with which you dealt unsuccessfully with know-it-alls, they will be the first to explain how you could have handled it more effectively. Second, they tend to be self-focused. Often the word "I" plays a central role in their comments.

Strategy 3: Focus on collaboration.

Collaboration is an educational buzzword. Even individuals who would fail a collaboration test make it an integral part of their vocabulary. However, true collaboration is essential in establishing successfully collegial relationships. At the same time, some new administrators are afraid to be truly collaborative. Even though they may say they are, they worry that they will either lose their authority or be viewed as weak if they are fully collaborative.

Administrators who are truly collaborative do not just talk about it but actually believe in the process. They understand what decisions are appropriate for group input and recognize which they should make alone. They invite faculty to be actively involved in such areas as curriculum and professional development but are unlikely to include them in personnel matters. Rather than attempting to control discussions and decisions, true collaborators truly seek out and weigh their colleagues' opinions and, in the end, tend to make better decisions.

As a beginning administrator, the collaborative process can be very helpful when you are confronted by difficult employee or parent issues. You can significantly increase your effectiveness if you seek out the advice of your administrative colleagues before taking action. For example, if some parents are asking you to exclude a particular novel from the required reading list, by asking other administrators to weigh in on the problem, you can use their wisdom to avoid a poor decision that might otherwise exacerbate the issue.

Strategy 4: Encourage socialization.

Administrators who are competitive avoid socializing with colleagues unless they perceive that it will somehow enhance their position with central office administrators, board members, or other employees. If you want to be viewed as part of the administrative team, you should be open to socializing outside work hours and even suggest getting together for lunch, dinner, or other activities. Remember that sometimes others might be waiting for someone else to initiate an event.

However, if you do take the lead, make sure you are inclusive. That is, invite everyone, even an administrator who is perceived as self-focused or competitive. Collaborative events become competitive and self-defeating once individuals are excluded. Most administrators want to be part of a group and value these types of supportive relationships.

Strategy 5: Always speak highly about your district and other administrators.

You must remember that what you say can help or hurt you. Always speak highly of your school district and colleagues. When you do, your comments will have a way of filtering back to others.

Similarly, if you make disparaging comments, they too tend to surface. One way those seeking administrative positions fall into this trap is by criticizing their current district or superintendent during the administrative interview process. A good rule of thumb is never to say anything about another administrator to anyone that you would not say to the person's face. In particular, never tell someone else anything about a colleague "in confidence." Think for a moment how often you've had someone say to you, "Don't tell anyone else this because I was told this in confidence, but. . . ."

RELATIONSHIPS WITH ADMINISTRATORS
OUTSIDE YOUR SCHOOL DISTRICT

Since principals and their assistants have a somewhat limited pool of in-district administrators, establishing a network of colleagues in similar level positions can contribute to your success. Since out-of-district administrative colleagues are not directly connected to your district, they can be an invaluable resource, especially if you work in either a competitive district environment or a small school district.

You may want to consider the following strategies to begin to establish an out-of-district administrative network.

Strategy 1: Make it a regular practice to gather information or "test" ideas with a pool of out-of-district administrators.

As problems and issues surface, you will want to contact multiple colleagues to find out if they have dealt with similar issues and how they resolved them. For example, you might be approached by parents who are questioning the selection process for your gifted program. Rather than responding immediately, you could call various colleagues to see how they have handled similar problems. Then, armed with more information and even ideas you had never considered, you are in a better position to respond to the parents.

Strategy 2: Volunteer to serve on multidistrict or township committees.

Often, school districts in particular geographic areas maintain standing articulation groups around common needs. Typical foci include curriculum coordination, personnel employment, pre-K–12 articulation, and professional development. By volunteering to serve as your district or school representative, you not only enhance your own professional development but make personal connections with other administrators.

Strategy 3: Join professional organizations.

Most professional administrative organizations have state and local chapters. Although it is important to be very school focused during your initial administrative years, if you can find some time to minimally participate, either as an attendee or possibly as a committee member, you not only start to build your professional relationship base but also broaden your experiences.

Strategy 4: Offer to lead an initiative.

As you serve on various groups, inevitably something specific needs to be accomplished. This usually means that someone must take responsibility for much of the planning and implementation. For example, if you are part of a consortium of school districts planning to host grade-level and subject area curriculum coordination meetings, volunteer to manage the process. By stepping forward and offering your services, you can contribute positively to the

process while gaining valuable leadership experience and further enhancing your professional network.

SUMMARY

Establishing positive, productive relationships with your administrative colleagues is one key to early administrative success. This chapter has explored how to work effectively with superintendents, central office administrators, and other building-level colleagues, as well as administrators from other school districts. Also discussed were examples of things novice administrators do that enhance or inhibit their success. Specific strategies you can employ to build networks of productive administrative relationships were suggested.

· 6 ·

Establishing Yourself
as the School Leader

$\mathcal{H}$ow often have you heard that the primary role of the principal is instructional leadership? Everyone from school board members to superintendents, as well as staff members and parents, expects principals to be knowledgeable about curriculum, assessment, instructional best practices, school improvement, and more. In fact, district superintendents report that a critical factor considered in the selection of their principals is knowledge in the field (Kersten, 2006).

Since leadership is such a highly valued quality in a school leader, as a new administrator you can be assured that others, including the central office administrators, teachers, and even parents, will judge your effectiveness by how successfully you manage your school and lead school improvement efforts. This reality raises an important question for you as a novice administrator: how can you quickly establish yourself as the school leader?

To begin, you should understand that effective leaders must be perceived by staff and parents as open-minded individuals. You must be the type of leader who encourages faculty members to share their thoughts, suggestions, and even criticisms directly with you.

The least effective administrators are those who sequester themselves in their offices, avoid informal staff and parent contact, and begin sentences with "yes, but." Some require others to address them by their titles even in informal situations. Still others expect staff members to schedule appointments to see them through their administrative assistants. As a new administrator, it is important to remember that others must feel comfortable approaching you, or they will be reluctant to follow your lead.

Visualize for a moment various school administrators with whom you have worked throughout your career. Were they highly visible, motivated

individuals who looked for rather than shied away from opportunities to interact with people? How did they respond when either a teacher or parent offered a suggestion? Did they present themselves as more collegial or authoritarian?

If you were fortunate enough to work with administrators who excelled in these areas, you know that their first response to most stakeholders' suggestions or questions is to show interest and, if appropriate, encourage a follow-up conversation in the not too distant future. Even though they do not necessarily say yes to every request, those who approach them typically walk away feeling that they were heard and that the administrators are open to their ideas.

On the other end of the spectrum, you may have experienced some who responded quite differently. Too often their reaction to a suggestion was either an immediate explanation of why it would not work or a comment that it had been tried before without success. These administrators project a persona of lack of openness to change and are often perceived by constituents as poor communicators who "must always have things their way."

Think about how you would feel if you approached your principal or assistant principal with an idea and the first reaction was "no." By immediately rejecting people's ideas, you discourage input and send the message that staff suggestions are not welcome. You cannot be a truly successful school leader unless others see you as approachable and open. You need to be the type of leader who sees the glass as half-full rather than half-empty and validates, rather than rejects, others' ideas.

As you prepare for your first administrative position, now is the time to self-assess in the area of how you typically respond to others. As is true of most things in life, you will normally react to something today similarly to how you have in the past. This is a good indicator of what will likely be your natural response as a new administrator. If during self-reflection you discover that your normal tendency is to react more as a half-empty than half-full leader, you may want to consider developing a more open, less judgmental response style.

THINK BEFORE YOU ACT

To present yourself as an administrator who is open to ideas from staff, parents, and other administrators, avoid the temptation to make on-the-spot decisions too frequently. Administrators are usually "take charge" individuals whose first reaction to any problem is to offer a solution. They often thrive on

problem solving, which is certainly an important skill for some situations. For example, if a teacher approaches you with a simple request such as switching supervision responsibilities with a colleague for a day, a quick, direct response is appropriate.

However, when staff members pose more complex suggestions, simple responses may actually create more problems than they solve. For example, if a teacher suggests a way to improve the master schedule, an "on-the-spot" response is generally inappropriate. If you reject the idea too quickly, you send the message that you are closed to change. Teachers and parents can become quickly "turned off" by administrators who do not appear open to new ideas.

A better approach is to take some time before responding, even if you feel pressured by day-to-day responsibilities. Let people know that you are interested in hearing their ideas and want to find a few minutes to discuss them. Even if you know fairly quickly that an idea is probably unworkable, you will do more to enhance your personal leadership status by scheduling a time to have a conversation.

Also, remember to consult with others, as appropriate. As a new administrator, you may not be aware of potential conflicts that might be lurking or aware that certain issues have long and contentious histories. Too often, administrators just react on the spot, often because they are very busy. However, in the long run, such reactions can undermine their effectiveness as leaders.

REMEMBER THAT YOU ARE NOT THE "PLEASER"

One mistake new administrators sometimes make is thinking that all they have to do to succeed is to make everyone happy. If this is your goal, you will always fail. You cannot control the happiness of others. A successful principal knows that leadership is far more complex than keeping everyone happy. Too often, novice administrators try to please everyone, from staff to parents to students, in order to avoid conflict. Unfortunately, differences of opinion are natural outcomes of personal interaction.

An administrator who avoids unpopular decisions or abdicates decision making to others as a way to either please or deflect criticism may soon find that he or she is no longer viewed as the school leader. More often than not, these individuals become nothing more than figureheads with little real authority. Remember that a lack of decisiveness and laissez-faire behavior are not substitutes for strong leadership. Rather, successful leaders understand when, when not, and how much to assert themselves as decision makers.

UTILIZE TOP-DOWN LEADERSHIP

A common misconception about effective leaders is that they cannot ever employ a top-down leadership style. Some believe that top-down leadership is completely unacceptable today in public education. Well, maybe not. DuFour (2007) argues that leader-directed behavior actually is critical to successful leadership, especially in professional learning communities. He uses the terms "tight" and "loose" to describe two leadership approaches that most effective administrators apply regularly.

DuFour (2007) defines *tight* as being firm—that is, expecting that something must be done because it is important to do and cannot be left to the discretion of others. In contrast, he describes being *loose* as allowing others the autonomy to "run with it"—that is, take the lead. However, "loose" does not mean without direction. Effective leaders will set parameters within which others can make decisions. Although DuFour's focus was primarily related to the implementation of professional learning communities, the tight/loose leadership approach has wide applicability, especially for new administrators.

Consider for a moment how effective principals would be if they left every decision up to a vote of the faculty. Probably little if anything would get accomplished in a timely manner. So much time would be spent just trying to schedule meetings that the organization's decision making would grind to a halt.

Similarly, under group decision making, more often than not, certain individuals—including some with very different perspectives—fill the leadership void. Without the direction of a single leader, organizational focus and efficiency could be compromised. However, by applying DuFour's (2007) tight/loose approach as a beginning administrator, you can begin to establish yourself as an effective school leader.

An important principle to learn is when to be tight or loose. To understand this, ask yourself which decisions you should make and which should be delegated to others. An effective way to approach this decision is to consider whether you can actually live with potential decisions made by others.

For example, would you permit teachers to decide not to offer an annual schoolwide open house for parents? Could you support a faculty decision to eliminate all report cards in lieu of one end-of-the-year parent conference? Would you let the staff decide to change parent conferences to daytime hours only? The point here is that you must weigh the consequences of any potential decision that might emanate from group decision making before deciding whether to be tight or loose.

Of course, you may be tight about scheduling a fall open house but loose about its structure. You might be tight about providing parents with quarterly report cards but loose in allowing parents and teachers to recommend changes to the reporting system itself. You might be tight about scheduling a certain number of evening parent conference hours but allow some flexibility in the format.

However, you would always set certain parameters within which teacher groups can exercise their decision-making authority. For example, teachers might be allowed to structure the open house schedule, alter the grade reporting system, or adjust parent conference hours but they would have to take into account parent needs.

MAKE STUDENTS YOUR NUMBER 1 PRIORITY

Although it sounds like a cliché, ensuring that leadership decisions are made around the interests of students is very important. Too often, less effective administrators base many of their decisions on what is in their personal best interests or those of staff. This is not a surprise, since most veteran administrators would probably tell you that the sources of most of their day-to-day problems do not emanate from students but rather from adults. As a result, they often tend to focus more on adult priorities in order to avoid conflict and criticism.

This is sometimes not apparent to those outside education. For example, if you announce to family and friends that you have just been hired as a middle school principal, a common response is, "Wow, that is a tough age group. You will have your hands full." The reality, though, is that most of your time will not be spent dealing with students but rather responding to adult, usually teacher, issues.

One of the great challenges of educational leadership is changing the focus of teachers from themselves to children. Think about the school in which you work today. Have some of the teachers said that they are unhappy because they just cannot find a way to help certain students learn? Or do they find other reasons to explain why particular students are not performing well? For example, some faculty members may believe that poor student performance has been caused by the district's unwillingness to provide smaller class sizes or additional classroom support.

For decades, the nature of school cultures has been more adult focused than student focused. School administrators often perpetuate this tradition by spending a substantial portion of their time responding to teacher rather than student needs. Some critics of public education might even contend that the reason schools have so many academic pull-out programs and special education services is that educators have avoided the tougher task of focusing on student needs in favor of adults'.

As a new administrator, you might feel strongly about trying to change this culture. However, you do not want to enter the school as the "Lone Ranger," ready to address each injustice, especially the adult versus student issue, head on. This will quickly alienate staff. However, to assert your leadership, you can consider several strategies to make inroads toward establishing a student-centered school.

Strategy 1: Hire well.

As Collins (2001) said in his book *Good to Great: Why Some Companies Make the Leap . . . and Others Don't,* you have to "get the right people on the bus" (41). Yet, even as a teacher, you have probably seen multiple examples of faculty members who are tenured (or who will be soon) but who are solely "me" focused. Most often, these individuals are resistant to change and tend to blame others for their lack of teaching success.

The reality is that because of state teacher tenure laws or collective bargaining provisions, these types of individuals will more often than not be employed in your district until they choose to leave. As a result, you must be committed to doing whatever it takes to employ new faculty members who share your desire to put children first and who also see helping students succeed as their primary responsibility.

Strategy 2: Set high standards for the reemployment of nontenured teachers.

Reemployment, and subsequently tenure, should never be automatic. One of the reasons that schools have poor teachers is that administrators have avoided dismissing below average nontenured teachers. Often, it was easier to avoid the potential political fallout of dismissal by lowering the standards for reemployment. Also, sometimes good is not good enough. You may need to actually expect those you rehire to be better than good.

Many individuals enter education because they want to make a difference. However, after they become administrators, they may find that decisions to dismiss employees often run counter to their natural tendencies to encourage and support. Today, though, administrators are recognizing more than ever just how critical it is to evaluate new teacher performance more objectively and not shy away from difficult employment decisions. A good test you might use to help you decide whether to reemploy a nontenured teacher is to ask yourself this simple question: would you employ this teacher today for a vacancy, given what you know about the teacher?

As an administrator, if a teacher has substantial performance problems, especially related to personality and professional commitment, you must recognize that these will likely worsen over time. Remember, beginning teachers can improve student management or teaching skills, but not a negative attitude.

Strategy 3: Make professional development a priority.

If schools and ultimately student achievement are to improve, teachers must have the knowledge and requisite instructional skills to perform well. One of the responsibilities of an effective school leader is creating a schoolwide learning environment for faculty members.

Historically, professional development has at times taken a backseat to daily teaching in some schools because there just does not seem to be enough time in the day to do everything that must be done. As a result, professional development is more often scheduled when time is available rather than when it would be most effective. If you think about your personal staff development experiences, more often than not these sessions were held either during isolated institute days when your focus was on preparing for classes or as you were approaching a vacation break. Many were probably generic in focus and not linked to your individual needs. In some cases, actual programs may have been "one shot" sessions or quick presentations by consultants.

To make professional development successful, you may want to consider the following suggestions.

- Be a catalyst for professional development.
  Effective administrators "walk the walk." Through their everyday actions, they show that they are knowledgeable about the latest best practices and issues in the field. They also encourage regular conversation with teachers around professional issues.

  They drop into classrooms during nonteaching times and attend grade-level and content-area meetings, where they have both informal and formal conversations about teaching and learning. These types of administrators often earn a reputation in the school and the district as curriculum leaders.
- Be "tight" about professional development.
  Some principals tend to be nondirective and make professional development secondary to day-to-day activities. Teachers will interpret any lack of principal interest as a message that professional development is not a priority.

As a new administrator, you need to make professional development an integral element of your school community by playing an active role in promoting a professional development plan. It is important to be "tight" about the value of professional development but "loose" about the details—as long as you establish that any initiatives must advance the mission and/or goals of the district or school. That is, set expectations for consistent, worthwhile, focused staff development, but allow teachers to impact the delivery model, selection of activities and presenters, and schedule.

- Align professional development with district priorities.

Successful school leaders see themselves as members of the district team. As such, they recognize that some school goals must align with district initiatives. Thus, they are "firm" about this expectation and work with faculty members to ensure that a portion of their school goals contributes to districtwide priorities.

- Make teachers an integral part of professional development planning and delivery.

For lasting change to occur, others must "buy in." Consider for a moment school or district professional development initiatives that were forgotten within a few months. Why did this occur?

For a change to become institutionalized, a critical mass of the staff must get on board. A principal can schedule an interesting professional development activity, but its impact will be minimal if teachers do not perceive any need. Teachers may politely participate, but little of substance will emerge if teachers do not see a need.

To increase the likelihood that professional development will make a difference, invite all faculty members directly into the planning and implementation process. In fact, a substantial portion of the faculty members must be involved if it is to have any lasting impact. You can increase your success rate even further if you include one or more of the normally resistant teachers.

A reality of public education is that teachers listen to teachers. If enough teachers are behind something, the odds of it succeeding increase dramatically. If you make yourself part of this team, you enhance your school leadership image.

- Avoid manipulating professional development planning.

Teachers see right through administrators who are disingenuous. One way to lose the respect of the faculty is to attempt to manipulate the school's professional development committee. Although you may have strong feelings about the focus of staff development, remember that effective school leaders express these feelings through the committee process rather than by attempting to manipulate committee decisions through individual team members.

At the same time, you can increase your effectiveness as a leader by giving a "charge," that is, by setting a direction for professional development. School leaders must provide a focus for professional development while allowing teachers latitude to plan. This will increase both the efficiency and effectiveness of any staff development planning process.

• Recognize that new learning takes time to become institutionalized. Change in public education is littered with failures. Do you remember whole language, minimal competency testing, or values clarification? These were popular topics for relatively short periods of time that never had a truly lasting effect.

To effect substantial change, you must expect that it will take time. Schools or school districts who focus on fewer, rather than more, improvement efforts over multiple years will potentially achieve more.

To be a successful school leader, avoid the temptation to define success in staff development and school improvement by the number of annual goals you identify or how many changes you can make quickly. Rather, work with faculty on a small number of foci, then create a multiyear implementation plan.

Strategy 4: Honor the decisions made by your predecessor.

As you assume your position, remember that you inherit school goals established by your predecessor. In many instances, faculty members and even parents may have had a part in their development. You can undermine your success quite early by immediately criticizing these and changing the school's agenda. A better approach is to recognize the importance of honoring past processes and slowly asserting your own ideas as the school year unfolds.

Strategy 5: Don't force your agenda.

Another mistake beginning administrators make is believing that they have all the answers and always know what is best. To impress their superintendents, they immediately make changes they perceive as critical, even within the first few weeks. They forget that to succeed, they must use both the "tight" and "loose" leadership approaches.

As a leader, you must have opinions. The difference, though, between successful and unsuccessful leaders is how they present them. Effective leaders are never afraid to state their ideas and challenge those of others, but they do not do so by using a supervisor-supervisee approach. They become personally involved in professional development without forcing their agendas on teachers.

More importantly, they immerse themselves as members of the decision-making team. For example, if your school is considering changing the overall student behavior management plan, an ineffective approach would be to dictate the new model. Successful principals or assistants form school committees on which they serve as members and where they participate more in the role of colleague than that of supervisor. They can still provide the organization and structure without forcing their personal agendas.

SUMMARY

This chapter has examined how beginning administrators can position themselves to be effective school leaders and truly make a difference within their schools. Included was a discussion of how school leaders can present themselves as open-minded while encouraging a productive schoolwide professional dialogue. Specific strategies new administrators can use to establish themselves as well-respected school leaders were presented.

· 7 ·

Managing Your School's Budget

*M*ost new administrators have minimal experience in school finance. As teachers, their focus was primarily on curriculum development, instructional planning, student supervision, and extracurricular activities. Other than recognizing that they will approve purchase requisitions, monitor school materials allocations, or manage various student funds, most beginning administrators are relatively unaware of their exact school-finance responsibilities. As a result, they often perceive their building-level responsibilities for school finance to be much more complex than they actually are.

Also, and maybe more importantly, they may not realize how critical proper management of even limited school funds can be to their success. Even though the amount of time actually spent on school budget-related activities is somewhat limited, a mismanagement of funds or a lack of sound fiscal policies and procedures could result in consequences as severe as dismissal. To avoid such school finance pitfalls, it is important for you to understand how to manage your school finance responsibilities.

DISTRICT BUDGETING METHODS

Before discussing how to manage school funds, understanding which method of budget development your school district employs is important. The two most common are the *zero-based* and *allocation-based* budgeting models.

Zero-Based Budgeting

Few districts today operate under the pure zero-based budgeting model, but many incorporate some of its basic principles when developing the district and school budgets. In theory, under this approach, the dollars allocated for each year's budget are not automatically set, but rather are based on specific needs. As a result, principals are expected by their superintendents to "make a case" for requested budget funds.

This approach was popularized in the 1970s but is rarely used exclusively today for budget development. Superintendents and business managers are more likely to employ a zero-based approach for a portion of the budget, generally for expenditures that the district does not annually budget. Typically, principals receive a basic school allocation and are expected to document why they need additional funds. Zero-based budgeting makes practical sense, especially for nonreoccurring expenditures, since almost all school districts today have limited revenues and must set distribution priorities.

Allocation–Based Method

A much more common budget approach is the allocation method. Under this model, principals receive a specific school allocation. The amount is adjusted annually, usually by a specific percentage based on the financial condition of the district and school or district priorities.

There are two predominant allocation-based methods. Under the first, principals receive a single building allocation, which they distribute among all building subaccounts. They usually have been given the discretion to distribute funds among departments, grade levels, and program areas as needed.

Through the second method, principals receive an allocation based on some fixed formula. For example, they may be allocated $20.00 for each student in kindergarten through third grade and $15.00 per student for grades 4 through 6. Separate amounts may be identified for specials such as physical education, music, and art.

The budgeting method and accompanying procedures that districts select vary depending on the size and location of the school district as well as the budgeting philosophy of the superintendent or school board. When you accept a position, it is important for you to understand your finance responsibilities and investigate your school district's budgeting approach.

Here are some strategies you can use to familiarize yourself with the budgeting process.

Strategy 1: Meet with your predecessor.

No one is more familiar with the specific budgeting process of the district and school than the person you replace. Spend some time "picking your predecessor's brain." However, you also want to ensure that your predecessor was a good manager. You will want to be careful not to follow the advice of anyone who left because of poor management. In these instances, you may want to seek out another principal for budget process information.

Strategy 2: Do not reinvent the wheel.

You always want to examine any budget reports, such as online or paper-copy documents. Also, review available district or school budget-related memos. Many budget tasks are completed similarly year after year. By reviewing past practices, you can develop a better understanding of how your school budget is structured and managed.

Strategy 3: Remember that the business manager is your friend.

The business manager or, if you are in a small district, the superintendent is responsible for the overall budget. The success of central office administrators is, in part, dependent on how well they manage school district finances. The last thing they want to do is deal with an avoidable budget mismanagement issue. Shortly after you assume your position, you should schedule a meeting with the business manager to review your responsibilities and seek advice on how you can best meet district expectations. You will also discover that business managers will look out for principals' interests, especially if they work well together.

Strategy 4: Recognize that your school's "real" budget expert may be your school secretary.

As a building administrator, you will be extremely busy. Wise administrators recognize what is a good use of their time and what is not. As a result, they often delegate to one of the office staff members most day-to-day budget management tasks. Office personnel, often the school secretary, enter purchase requisitions, check in items as they are received, advise staff on building and district procedures, and follow up with staff on business office questions. As a result, your secretary can provide you with valuable advice about your school's budgeting procedures.

Experienced administrators also know that their secretaries and office clerks usually have their fingers on the pulse of the school. If you consult them on budget matters and include them as part of the budget management team, they will be more likely to alert you to potential problems before they become crises.

BUDGET MANAGEMENT

Once you have investigated your district and school budgeting model and corresponding procedures, you must turn your attention to budget management. Your goal is to ensure that you handle all budget responsibilities seamlessly, efficiently, and honestly. Below are several strategies you can employ to help ensure your success.

Strategy 1: Establish procedures and timelines to manage the flow of business office communication.

School districts have a plethora of business office forms and procedures that are important for the efficient management of the district. Since the office staff generally manages district procedures, you want to ensure that they are fully trained.

An effective approach is to designate an individual or individuals who are responsible for business functions. These include

- submitting purchase requests;
- checking in received items;
- submitting check requests;
- managing field-trip requests;
- cross-checking employee absence forms;
- monitoring hourly employee timesheets;
- processing maintenance and technology help requests.

Strategy 2: Monitor budget expenditures regularly.

Before you assumed your position, your predecessor developed the school budget that you now must administer. Your primary responsibility is to ensure that you do not exceed budgeted amounts in any area. You also must ensure that you maintain adequate funds for second semester needs. For example, if you will incur June graduation expenses, you will need to make sure that funds are kept in reserve rather than expended on other items during the year.

To monitor budget expenses effectively, you should commit to studying your school budget accounts at least monthly. Depending upon your school district's level of technology, either these will be online or they will be found in district-generated reports. They will show you the amount allocated in each account. They will also include encumbered expenses, that is, purchase orders issued but not yet processed, and current account balances.

Strategy 3: Authorize your office personnel to monitor staff expenditure requests.

Since office staff members manage most daily budget tasks, you can add an extra layer of budget oversight by delegating to them responsibility for reviewing the appropriateness of staff expenditure requests. They can serve as "first line" supervisors by identifying any questionable requests. However, they should be expected to bring any unusual requests to you for approval. If your staff feel a greater sense of responsibility for school funds and are invited to ensure that expenditures are appropriate, you will decrease the likelihood of inappropriate use of funds.

Strategy 4: Set expenditure limits for all accounts.

To minimize overspending surprises, you should establish an expenditure limit for all school-budget line items. When any department, grade level, or program area exceeds the limit, an automatic review is triggered. An 80 percent expenditure/encumbrance level is a reasonable trigger point.

Strategy 5: Maintain an administrative contingency fund.

No matter how organized and efficient you are, you can never anticipate the unexpected. As a result, as you prepare future budgets, set aside a certain amount of your building allocation for unpredictable expenses. If you discover later that no one anticipated that you would need textbooks for ten new students, you will have funds available.

Strategy 6: Understand your district's policy on shifting funds between building accounts.

In almost every school, some departments or grade levels run short of funds while others never use all their allocation. However, before deciding to shift funds from one account to another, make sure you know your school district's policy. This is especially important in your first year, when you want to avoid poor decision making. Some districts allow you to exceed your budgeted amount in one account as long as the overall budget remains within its total allocation. Others will require approval from the central office.

Strategy 7: Reaffirm your budget management expectations and procedures with faculty and staff.

As a new administrator, it is important for you to articulate clearly your budget management expectations and procedures. Faculty and staff are accustomed to those of the previous administration. You can avoid confusion and increase schoolwide efficiency if you clearly delineate your building procedures and expectations from the start of the school year. This should be an item on your first faculty/staff meeting agenda.

Strategy 8: Establish a "no cash" policy.

Although the use of cash in schools is unavoidable, you can eliminate a plethora of potential problems by discouraging its use and regulating how faculty and staff manage money. Have you ever been in a school in which a teacher collected field-trip money and left it in a desk drawer at night, only to discover it missing in the morning? Have you ever heard of principals being questioned about how they used money from special "slush funds" kept in school safes? These actions create ethical and even legal issues.

To minimize these problems, always expect employees to turn in any cash collected to the school office daily. If at all possible, arrange to have funds transferred to the business office as soon as possible. Avoid locking the money in the school safe or file cabinet for any period of time.

In addition to discouraging employees from holding money, ensure that you create a paper trail for all cash. Some employees will be tempted to use money collected from students or school activities for cash purchases. Although the purchases may be legitimate, the use of cash increases the opportunity for misuse of funds or the appearance of misuse.

A better approach is to require employees to turn in all funds to the school office and use approved purchasing procedures for all expenditures. By requiring staff to follow approved procedures, you can assess the appropriateness of all expenditures and document the use of funds.

All school districts have in place specific procedures for ordering and accounting for purchases. Many still employ traditional purchase orders. However, procurement cards, which function similarly to credit cards but with specific limits, are becoming more common. They also decrease paper flow and increase efficiency.

Strategy 9: Monitor spring spending.

In some schools, spring means "spend." Employees who have budget funds remaining often decide to spend rather than lose them. This can result in the purchase of many unnecessary items. It can also send the wrong message to the district administration and school board. Most superintendents discourage their principals from allowing this practice. They may even interpret this as an indication that the school's budget allocation was too high. Board members may express similar views when they review a large number of late-year expenditures.

As a beginning administrator, you want to alert faculty and staff to this problem. If your district does not have a specific end-of-the-year expenditure cutoff date, set one for your school. March 1 is a reasonable date. Exceptions can be made for needs which emerge later in the school year.

Strategy 10: Ensure that any new school revenue initiatives are approved by central office staff.

One sure way that new administrators can find themselves in difficulty is by authorizing a fund-raising activity without understanding the implications. Approving an innocent request from the cheerleading club sponsor to sell candy during lunch periods to raise funds for new pompoms might lead to district-wide controversy. Although on the surface the activity seems innocuous enough, you would be violating the National School Lunch Program junk food ban if you approved it.

Similarly, if you allowed your food service vendor to conduct a raffle to increase lunch revenues, you could get an unwelcome reaction. For example, how might parents and teachers react to a raffle in which students who purchased a school lunch received a raffle ticket for an expensive bicycle?

Whenever you are approached with any revenue-raising request, it is good practice to discuss it with central office administrators prior to making a decision. They can help you consider all the ramifications. More importantly, they can keep you from "shooting yourself in the foot."

ACTIVITY FUNDS

The first part of this chapter focused on school budget expenditures linked to the overall school district budget. However, school level administrators also manage activity funds.

Activity funds differ from regular school budget funds in two ways. First, activity funds are used to account for revenues and expenditures associated with nondistrict funds. No taxes are deposited in activity fund accounts. Second, activity funds are used to manage funds collected by clubs, activities, and special groups such as individual school faculties or parent organizations.

School districts usually maintain a single activity fund with separate accounts for schools, which are further divided into school subaccounts. It is common for a school to have subaccounts for such areas as student clubs or the staff. Does your school have a "coffee" account through which teachers collect money for coffee and soda and use the proceeds to replenish their beverage supply as necessary?

Although the district activity fund and school subaccounts are segregated from district funds, they too are audited during the school district's regular annual audit. They also are subject to specific legal regulations governing their use. The total dollars in the activity funds are relatively low when compared to those in the overall school district budget. However, auditors are always concerned about activity funds because the fraud risks are relatively high.

As a new administrator, you need to be aware that you are administratively responsible for managing your school activity fund accounts. You must not only sign activity fund check requests but also approve their appropriateness.

You can easily damage your career by failing to monitor your school's activity accounts. If, for example, funds from a student club are used for some other purpose, you open yourself up to political and credibility problems. This is one area you want to monitor closely to maintain your credibility.

To minimize potential activity fund issues, you may want to consider the following practices.

- Require employees to receive preapproval, in writing if at all possible, for all expenditures.
- Review and sign off on each expenditure request to ensure appropriateness.
- Request review assistance from district office personnel for any expenditure about which you have any questions.
- Expect that all funds collected by various groups will be deposited in the appropriate activity fund account.
- Require written, detailed receipts for all expenditures.
- Reinforce with your staff the importance of managing all funds ethically.

SUMMARY

This chapter focused on school-building administrators' school finance responsibilities. Discussed were the two most common school district budgeting methods: zero-based and allocation-based. Specific strategies were offered, which novice administrators might use to familiarize themselves with both the district and school budgeting processes. Also suggested were strategies new administrators could employ successfully to manage their school budgets.

Finally, the nature and purpose of school activity funds were discussed. Included was a discussion of the role of building administrators in activity fund account management. Specific suggestions were offered to help new administrators avoid potential activity fund pitfalls.

· 8 ·

Making Teacher Selection and First Year Teacher Evaluation Top Priorities

*P*ublic education is a people-centered business. Selecting and retaining the most effective teachers is crucial to the success of the school and the success of school administrators. As a result, probably the most important responsibility influencing an administrator's long-term success is selecting high-performance faculty members.

TEACHER SELECTION

Effective teachers make all the difference in the quality of a student's educational experience. Since student learning is the primary focus of the school, and teachers are the central figures in students' school lives, the teaching staff can make or break both the school's success and yours as the building administrator.

Unfortunately, when you accept your first administrative position, you inherit rather than select your faculty members. How effective your teachers are depends on how well administrators over past thirty-plus years have hired and supervised.

Even though you had no direct control over who was previously hired, you generally have much more authority to select future teachers. As a result, you would be served well to make teacher selection one of your top priorities from the moment you begin your new administrative position.

Although every school has many excellent faculty members, they also have some who are either difficult to work with or ineffective in the classroom. As a beginning administrator, you will easily be able to identify both your top performers and problem employees in a very short period of time.

In fact, either the former principal or a central office administrator may even "fill you in" on teachers they valued and those about whom they had concerns. The reality is that, shortly after starting your first administrative position, you will also find yourself gravitating to the "stars" and wondering why the poor performers were hired initially or, more critically, why they were retained.

There is no single reason why schools have ineffective teachers. Rather, a variety of factors may have produced this result. However, one of the most common is that former administrators may not have made teacher selection and evaluation high enough priorities.

Too often principals and their assistants become overwhelmed with all the demands of their positions. As they are true "managers in the middle," a substantial number of their daily responsibilities emanate from the actions of central office administrators, staff members, parents, and students. Most spend a great deal of their time responding to issues and problems created by others. Unfortunately, because of these problems and issues, some of which are very conflict based and time sensitive, teacher hiring can slide down the list of priorities.

Another reason average or below average teachers are employed initially is a lack of quality applicants. For years, teacher shortages in certain teaching areas have plagued both public and private schools. In fact, both the Bureau of Labor Statistics (BLS, 2009) and the American Association for Employment in Education (2009) report a shortage of teachers in areas such as bilingual education, special education, mathematics, and science.

The BLS (2009) projects that this trend will continue through 2016. In fact, even in school districts which often have little difficulty attracting candidates, the applicant pool is predicted to be smaller. Shortages will be especially acute in urban and rural school districts as well as those with lower teacher salaries, larger class sizes, and low pupil spending (Kersten, 2008). Each of these factors points to the necessity of making teacher hiring a top priority.

As a school leader, you must work hard to ensure that hiring well is your number 1 priority. Since every hire is key, you do not want to shortcut any phase of the hiring process. Remember that with every person you hire, you leave your legacy. Therefore, if you want to increase the number of "good hires," consider committing additional time to hiring and also using a more comprehensive teacher selection process.

BUILDING THE APPLICANT POOL

Did you ever work in a school in which the principal did not begin hiring teachers until the school year ended in June? Some administrators will postpone hiring until they are "out from under" the demands of the school year. They rationalize their timing by thinking that there will be an abundance of good candidates available when they finally have time to interview.

Unfortunately, this logic is flawed. Most successful administrators know that the best candidates are "snapped up" early. They also recognize that even though the candidate pool may appear to have sufficient applicants, only a small percentage are truly excellent. Therefore, a first step toward improving teacher candidate quality is attracting more applicants.

One key to expanding your applicant pool and increasing the number of top candidates is to start early and "leave no stone unturned." Some administrators rely almost exclusively on candidates they know (teacher assistants, substitutes, or those recommended by staff). Others assume that those interested will submit their applications without prompting.

Such recruiting approaches mean that you will attract only those who are somehow connected to the school or who have applied by coincidence. Many strong candidates who might be interested, if they were familiar with your district, never apply.

Remember, you can never have too many candidates from whom to choose. But you *can* find yourself with no good option for a particular position if you are not an aggressive recruiter. To build the largest candidate pool possible, consider the following strategies.

Strategy 1: Begin your search early.

Although you may not yet be able to identify all your vacancies, this should not deter you from beginning your recruiting in January. One key to attracting a large number of applicants is to get in the market early. You should start by advertising actual openings as well as potential vacancies.

Strategy 2: Know how to reach the best candidates.

Unlike years ago when teacher candidates "blanketed the area" with their resumes, today many are more selective. Colleges of education no longer recommend such paper-intensive approaches. Also, applicants are generally expected to do much more than mail in a resume. Today, school districts require more information and regularly expect candidates to provide detailed responses to several questions. As a result, some candidates, especially those in low-supply areas such as special education, ESL, or the sciences, may limit the number of districts to which they apply rather than completing numerous complex applications.

Also, candidates today are more likely to use the Internet to locate positions. Traditional university placement office newsletters have been replaced by Web postings through university, county, professional associations, and school district websites.

As a result, do not overlook your own school district website. Some candidates will target certain areas or even particular schools where they hope to apply. You want to ensure that your openings are easy to find on your district website and that links to the application process are readily accessible and easy to use. Also, consider including positive information about your district, such as student performance data, salary schedules, class size averages, and amount of dollars spent per child, which will further attract candidates.

In addition, you will want to familiarize yourself with every possible Web-based recruiting source in your market area. By developing a comprehensive list of Web-based sources through which you can post vacancies, you can easily begin recruiting with just a quick e-mail. By listing your openings through available websites, you can reach thousands of potential candidates in a matter of minutes.

Although technology can increase the efficiency of your recruiting, it can also be a deterrent. Some school districts adopt such extensive, time-consuming Web-based application processes that candidates avoid them. The key is finding a balance, measuring how long or complex your online application is against what information you truly need.

A useful question that your district's administrative team may want to discuss is, "How can we develop a simple, concise application process that encourages candidates to apply and gives us the information needed to identify qualified candidates?" Remember that a user-friendly application process will yield more candidates.

Do not overlook the efficacy of job fairs. In many areas, school districts, consortia of districts, universities, and professional associations sponsor job fairs. These represent an excellent way to build a large candidate pool for specific and potential openings.

Job fairs can be overwhelming for both employers and candidates. However, with some planning, you can increase their usefulness as a recruiting tool. Here are several ways to improve the effectiveness of job fair recruiting.

- Select a district team to conduct the interviews.
- Limit interviews to five minutes.
- Create a positive public relations information sheet about your school and district to distribute.
- Train team members on what to ask, the qualifications and personal qualities to consider, and how to make a snap judgment.

- Do not be too discriminating. Try to identify a larger rather than smaller pool of potential "yes" candidates. They can be screened later to narrow the applicant pool.
- Have written information available for candidates on how to complete the application process.
- Schedule a meeting with interview team members as soon as possible after they return from the job fair to identify the most viable candidates for further consideration.
- Make sure you identify promising candidates even in areas where you presently do not have a vacancy. You never know when someone may submit a resignation.

Strategy 3: Ramp up your networking.

Some very good teachers are successfully recruited through personal networking. If your goal is an expansive candidate pool, encourage other administrators, teachers, support staff, and even friends to recommend candidates. They may know a future "superstar" who might otherwise never apply.

However, here is one word of caution: be prepared to "meet and greet" a large number of candidates. Have you ever recommended someone for a position in your district, and the person was never invited for even a brief screening interview? One way to build political support is to take the time to ensure that anyone with some connection to you or the district is interviewed at least briefly. Also, you may receive advice from other administrators and board members. You want to make sure you listen willingly.

EMPLOYING A COMPREHENSIVE SELECTION PROCESS

Teachers should almost never be hired after merely a brief interview with the principal. Furthermore, the decision should never be based on a "gut" reaction. Probably one of the least defensible statements an administrator can make to the superintendent on why to hire a particular individual is, "I liked that candidate."

Hiring is not about liking a person. Rather, it is about recruiting and selecting the most outstanding individual after gathering as much data as possible. In essence, you are predicting who will ultimately be the best person for the position. Remember that even with an elaborate process, there is no guarantee that you will make the right decision. However, you increase your success rate significantly if your decision is the result of a multifaceted selection process.

Once you have identified a strong candidate pool, the really hard work begins. You must now get to know each candidate much better, especially the one to whom you will ultimately offer the position.

A good way to conceptualize the process is to picture a funnel. When you begin the selection process, your candidate pool is widest, as you consider a broad spectrum of candidates. As you move through each selection stage, the field is narrowed.

FIFTEEN-MINUTE INTERVIEW

At the early stages of the selection process, you want to meet as many candidates as possible. Too often, administrators will artificially narrow the candidate pool with too tight a screening process based primarily on written documents. To ensure that you do not eliminate too many potentially strong candidates based upon just their resumes or student teaching assignments, you want to set looser rather than tighter initial screening criteria.

Some student teachers have minimal control over where they student teach. Therefore, if you base your screening decision to a large extent on where someone previously taught, you can rule out individuals who may be quite talented. In fact, some excellent candidates with a year of two of experience may have accepted a position in a less desirable school district just to "get a foot in the door." To control for this variable, you would be well served to screen a broad cross section of potential teachers.

A mistake some administrators make is conducting lengthy screening interviews. If you schedule candidates for thirty-minute interviews, you will be unable to consider as many as you would if you limited first interviews to fifteen minutes. As a result, you may never meet the best person.

Veteran principals will tell you that they can often make a screening decision on a candidate's viability in just a few minutes. If you have scheduled thirty-minute interviews, you will find yourself wasting a substantial amount of precious time.

The purpose of the fifteen-minute interview is quite simple. It is to answer the question, "Is this individual someone I could possibly see teaching in our district?" In essence, you are making a yes/no decision.

At this stage, the "yes" criteria should be fairly loose. You want to review the person's personal and professional background and decide whether the individual's personality may be appropriate for your school. Those who pass this simple test move on to the next level. However, always let candidates know that the interview will only be fifteen minutes, so they do not interpret a brief interview as a poor one.

SECOND INTERVIEW

As an outcome of the screening interview process, the candidate pool is generally cut at least in half. Those who are not a good match are quickly eliminated. Make sure that you contact these candidates to let them know their status. You can damage your reputation if you let them wait, rather than informing them that they are out of consideration.

Although these interviews can be conducted by the principal alone, it is more effective to invite others, such as central office administrators, other principals, assistant principals, deans, and other certificated support personnel into the process. The more opinions you consider, the more likely it is that you will make the best hiring decision.

With administrative experience, you will discover one hiring phenomenon: some individuals are more successful in selecting the best candidates. Although it is nearly impossible to quantify this skill, some administrators are just better at teacher selection. What you may want to consider is whether you are one of these individuals. You may not even be able to self-assess your skills at first. However, until you have a hiring track record, you can invite other district administrators, especially those with a reputation for hiring well, to assist with interviewing.

The second interview is typically thirty to forty-five minutes. It should be focused on further assessing the match between the candidate and the school, and how well prepared the candidate is. You want to understand what candidates truly believe about student learning and their craft. As a result, the interview questions should shift from broad to more specific and situation based.

Asking someone to "tell me what middle school students are like" provides little useful information. Asking "Why did you go into teaching?" only produces a clichéd response. If you really want to get to know candidates, you must be more direct. You need to focus on what candidates have accomplished and what they believe. Some more effective questions to ask candidates include the following:

- Describe a personal experience that had an impact on your teaching.
- How would you facilitate communication between home and school?
- What would your worst critic say about you?
- How important is it for you to be liked by your students?
- Describe a typical class period.
- What instructional strategies have you found most effective?
- Describe a lesson that was particularly successful, and walk me through each stage, from planning to delivery.

- Explain what a strong, balanced literacy program would look like in your classroom.
- What research-based teaching strategies have you used?
- What specific strategies would you use to assist students who are struggling in reading or mathematics?
- What do you do when you see someone is not learning?
- What do you do with students who continually fail to complete homework?
- Describe the toughest discipline problem you ever encountered, and explain how you handled it.
- If you were having classroom management problems, when would you ask for help, and to whom would you direct the request?
- Describe the best lesson you ever taught, and explain why it was great.
- Describe a challenge you encountered during student teaching. What did you learn from it?
- If you were doing something for your students that you knew was right and your principal told you to stop, what would you do?
- Describe a lesson that did not go particularly well, and explain how you used this to improve your teaching.
- Is there anything I didn't ask you that you hoped I would?

You should also avoid the "I really like this person" syndrome. Too often, administrators equate their positive personal connections with candidates with teaching knowledge and skill. If you invite others to participate in interviews, you can minimize the tendency to make personality-based hiring decisions.

During this interview, you will find it helpful to encourage candidates to ask questions at the end. What they ask can provide you with significant insights into what they value and their priorities.

FINAL INTERVIEW

After you complete the second round of interviews, your candidate pool should be significantly narrowed. At this point, you have screened and interviewed candidates and are ready to select your finalists.

As a new administrator, you will soon discover that no candidate is perfect. However, as the employer, you want to make sure you really know the person you are hiring. As a result, it is good practice to conduct a third interview with those you consider finalists.

The final interview allows you to ratchet up your expectations by asking probing questions focused on topics that may have been only touched on, or not even discussed, during pervious interviews. It also provides you an opportunity to see whether candidates are still presenting accurate and consistent pictures of themselves.

REFERENCE CHECKING

In conjunction with the final interview, an essential selection process step is conducting reference checks. Oftentimes, this step is overlooked or underappreciated. Reference checks should include both formal and informal sources.

As part of the application process, each candidate should have been asked to supply you with a list of references. This should, at a minimum, include immediate supervisors. For those who have only student taught, their cooperating teachers and university supervisors are their most direct references. They have observed the candidate in action and can provide the most detailed and specific perspectives. However, in some instances, the principal or assistant principal may also be a reference.

Simultaneously, use informal reference checks. That is, contact individuals who are not on the candidate-supplied reference list. Since school administrators usually have wide personal networks, a few well placed calls can yield some "off the record" candidate assessments.

Also, you have to use your judgment when assessing the value of a particular reference. Not all will be forthright. Some may hold back information, deflect questions, or only provide glowing comments. This is why you should contact multiple reference sources, including informal ones.

Informal reference checks can help you gauge more accurately a candidate's true performance. School office staff members such as receptionists and school secretaries can provide unsolicited candidate appraisals. You might be surprised how candid they can be!

DOCUMENTING REFERENCE CHECKS

Somewhere in your lifetime, you probably have heard of a teacher who was hired and later turned out to have a "dark" past. In some instances, the teacher may have been hired without a reference check. Picture yourself in the midst of a scandal, being asked by your school board during a closed session why you did not know that the person was forced to resign elsewhere for a similar reason.

Although the likelihood of this occurring is remote, it is prudent to anticipate such a problem. An effective technique is to create a simple form that you complete each time you conduct a reference check. On the form, you document whom you contacted, when, and the relationship to the candidate. You also jot down a summary of reference comments. You should retain these forms in the candidate's confidential personnel file as evidence of thorough reference checking. If at a later date you are confronted with a serious issue, you can at the least show your due diligence.

RECEPTIONIST REACTIONS

Another person who can provide you with a candidate perspective is the receptionist who greets interviewees. Receptionists often see a side of an individual that you may not see once the candidate enters the interview room. Because receptionists interact with candidates waiting for interviews, they can provide insights about how candidates act in informal settings. You can be assured that candidates will likely treat support staff members the same way they treat the receptionist.

DEMONSTRATION TEACHING

If you have followed each step of the process to date, you have probably narrowed your search to one to three candidates. In fact, you may be especially interested in one individual. However, if you make your hiring decision based on the information you have gathered to date, you are leaving out an important step in the teacher selection process. That is, you have yet to see the candidate work with students.

A highly effective next step is to require a demonstration teaching lesson. Although it is to some degree artificial, it will give you a sense of a candidate's natural teaching style and ability to relate to students. Remember that some candidates are excellent interviewers. They can "talk a good game." However, when you hire them, they turn out to be below-average teachers.

To minimize this potential problem, consider requiring the final candidate or two to teach a demonstration lesson. If you have them teach in your school, you can control for some of the unknown variables that might cloud the experience if you observed them in their own classrooms. You will also have a more objective gauge of their natural teaching skills.

To maximize the classroom teaching component, you may want to consider the following.

- Allow candidates to meet with the teacher in whose classroom the demonstration lesson will occur.
- Offer candidates the opportunity to either extend the regular classroom teacher's lesson or bring in their own.
- Invite at least one district administrator to join you for the observation.
- Utilize a preconference/observation/postconference observation model, which will permit you to assess the planning and self-evaluation skills of the candidates.

Demonstration teaching will help you judge how effective the teacher may be. Plus, you will confirm your judgments to date about the candidate's knowledge, skill, and personal qualities.

TEACHER INPUT

In conjunction with the demonstration-teaching component, it is good practice to invite some faculty members to interview the candidate. This not only allows them to participate in the process but provides you with additional perceptions. You should also provide them with parameters for participation and explain their role in the process.

One crucial mistake new administrators can make is not clearly delineating who will make the final hiring decision. Some mistakenly think that by allowing faculty members significant input early in the process or letting them make the final "hiring call," they are enhancing their leadership position.

The reality is that they are actually diminishing their authority. Teacher involvement is important. However, remember that this is one time you can have a major impact on the school's culture. If you allow teachers who want to maintain the status quo to select their new colleague, whom do you think they will choose? View this as your opportunity to begin establishing your vision for the school by employing individuals who share your vision.

If you make teacher hiring a top priority and implement a comprehensive selection process, you can truly improve the quality of your faculty hiring decisions. This is a crucial step in establishing yourself as an effective school leader while employing individuals who can help you contribute to school improvement efforts.

FIRST YEAR TEACHER EVALUATION

Now that you have hired your faculty members, your work has just begun. Schools have poor teachers not only because they did not place enough effort on the hiring process initially, but also because administrators did not thoroughly supervise new faculty members or make the difficult decision to dismiss below-average performers.

Almost no one enjoys telling teachers that they will not be reemployed. However, if nontenured teachers are ineffective in the classroom or difficult to work with, failure to dismiss them will create long-term problems for you and the school.

Furthermore, under either state teacher-tenure laws or collective bargaining agreements, school boards and administrators generally have great latitude in the reemployment of nontenured teachers. Although the specific legal requirements vary from state to state, the burden of proof required for the dismissal of nontenured teachers is generally minimal. However, once teachers are tenured, it is very difficult to dismiss them because of the extensive legal protections they enjoy.

As a new administrator, you cannot shy away from your supervision responsibilities, even if you feel discomfort or know that the dismissal will create political unrest. Rather, it is in your best interest and that of your students to set a high standard for teacher reemployment.

Most average or below-average teachers have performed at that level from the moment they were hired. Very few deteriorated dramatically later. Most were reemployed because their evaluating administrators were not effective supervisors.

In these instances, either the administrators did not thoroughly evaluate their nontenured teachers, or they simply chose to avoid the uncomfortable task of releasing them. Some may even have convinced themselves subconsciously that the teachers either had potential to be excellent or were actually performing well. When these administrators ultimately leave, their successors will inherit the problem employees, often for their entire careers.

JUDGING NOVICE TEACHER EFFECTIVENESS

One of the most difficult decisions you will make as an administrator is deciding whom to reemploy. Since you will often hire beginning teachers, most will need to gain experience before they achieve excellence. Consequently, during their first year or two teaching, you will more often be judging their potential for excellence rather than their current skills.

One way to assess their potential is to judge their ability to relate to others. Be aware that personality is usually extremely difficult to actually change. People are who they are. You can be assured that any teacher who has difficulty relating with others, displays a negative attitude, shows inflexibility, challenges authority, is inappropriately stern with students, or is overly opinionated will be that and more in years to come.

On the other hand, experienced administrators will tell you that teachers who may struggle initially with classroom management, instructional pacing, or teaching strategies, but who are otherwise self-reflective and have strong personal skills, may have potential.

One issue with which some administrators struggle is retaining teachers who are effective in the classroom but exhibit poor interpersonal skills. You should view this as a major "red flag." Have you ever heard administrators lament that they offered tenure to a particular teacher because the person was effective in the classroom, despite the fact that the teacher had relationship problems? Most have regretted this decision. Remember that a teacher's effectiveness must be judged on overall performance, not just what the teacher does in the classroom.

Another method to assess a candidate's potential consists of informal and formal observations, both in and out of the classroom. Before deciding to reemploy nontenured teachers, scrutinize all aspects of their performance. Below are specific strategies you may want to consider as part of the reemployment decision.

Strategy 1: Conduct extensive teacher observations.

You can never observe a new faculty member too often. In fact, as discussed in chapter 2, you want to begin informal drop-ins and mini-observations shortly after they begin teaching. Through these, you will be able to form some initial judgments. You will also be able to identify and perhaps address any potential problems early.

Strategy 2: Conduct formal observation cycles.

One of the most effective ways to determine if teachers are knowledgeable, skilled, and self-reflective is through the teacher observation process. This process begins with a preobservation conference, during which you discuss with the teacher all aspects of a lesson you will observe. The primary purpose of the preobservation conference is for you to develop an understanding of the context of the lesson and the teacher's instruction plan.

Following the preobservation conference, you observe not only the effectiveness of instruction but as much about the teacher as possible. You want to observe whether the teacher is able to implement the lesson plan. You also want to focus on the teacher's interactions with students, his or her classroom management skills, and even the physical environment.

As soon as possible following the observation, you should meet with the teacher to discuss all aspects of the lesson. During this session, you will be able to judge how self-reflective the teacher actually is. Since you will provide some constructive feedback, you will also be able to see how open the teacher is to suggestions. All this data can be ultimately factored into your reemployment decision.

Strategy 3: Invite other administrators in your school or even from the central office to observe nontenured teachers' classroom instruction.

A second set of eyes and another perspective will help inform your assessment. Too often administrators operate in a vacuum. If you are a beginning administrator, you may miss some important activity or even fail to focus on some important aspect of the observation. The more you collaborate with colleagues, especially during teacher observation, the more you will learn from them about effective supervision and the greater the likelihood that you will thoroughly vet the candidate.

Strategy 4: Observe the teacher in nonclassroom settings.

Because you want to retain teachers who are both effective in the classroom and are contributing faculty members, you must make a point of observing them throughout the day. This means observing how they relate in social and professional settings with students, colleagues, and parents. You can observe how they choose to use their planning time as well as their contributions in meetings. By viewing them outside their classrooms, you can develop a good sense of whether they are individuals with whom you want to work for years to come.

Strategy 5: Ask key support staff for their impressions of new teachers.

Often social workers, counselors, and special service personnel who work directly with students and their teachers see a side of the teacher you may not. They can tell you how someone performs when the administration is not there or a conflict is developing. This is valuable information that you can factor into your final assessment.

MAKING THE REEMPLOYMENT CALL

The bottom line is that as a school-level administrator, you will almost always be expected to make the reappointment recommendation. Although it may at first appear harsh, most veteran administrators would advise you to dismiss any nontenured teacher about whom you have any doubt. This is especially true with those who display poor people skills or lack good judgment. The risk-reward is too great. If you are make the wrong call, you will strap the district with a poor employee, potentially for decades.

Yet when making a dismissal call, you may have to be prepared for push-back from staff, parents, community members, and even board members. All employees begin to make personal connections from the moment they accept their positions. In most instances, this is a plus. However, when the person is either an ineffective or problem teacher, these connections may mean that your dismissal decision will create waves among some group. If these are minimal, they will pass quickly. But if the teacher has managed to build a support base, you may find yourself the center of a controversy.

The level of potential controversy increases the longer a teacher continues to be reemployed. If, for example, in your state, teacher tenure is awarded after four years, you substantially increase the potential for conflict if you wait until after the third or fourth year to dismiss. It is not unusual for groups of parents or teachers to demand to meet with you to share their unhappiness. Some may carry their concerns to the superintendent or school board directly.

Such conflicts can shift from the central issue of teacher performance to claims that you are terminating someone either because the teacher expressed views different from yours or from some hidden political motive. Unfortunately, you will find yourself in the position of not being able to discuss the teacher's performance with other employees and parents because it is a personal matter, while the teacher and supporters can say almost anything they choose about you.

As a result, it is advisable to first ensure that when you evaluate teachers, you link any concerns in the written evaluation to specific areas of the teacher evaluation document. You can ask your superintendent for help with this. Also, do not wait multiple years to dismiss. A teacher with significant personal or teaching problems will not likely improve much during the third or fourth years.

Principals and assistants who have experienced this process and made the tough call almost always feel vindicated the following school year. When they conduct the beginning-of-the-year faculty meeting and no longer have to worry about the problem employee, they realize that they have made the correct decision. However, be prepared to deal with a loss of popularity. This is one of the prices of strong leadership.

SUMMARY

This chapter has examined the critical importance of selecting high-performance teachers as well as thoroughly evaluating first year teachers. As part of the discussion, the reasons some ineffective teachers are often hired initially and even retained were explored.

Presented also was a comprehensive teacher selection process model that could be used to enhance a school district's teacher hiring process. This model included strategies that administrators could use to broaden their candidate pool, expand the number and quality of candidate interviews, and conduct more effective candidate reference checks. In addition, the importance of including a demonstration teaching component in the selection process was discussed.

Finally, the critical importance of evaluating both the classroom and nonclassroom nontenured teacher performance to retaining only the most effective nontenured teachers was analyzed. To build a highly competent and cohesive faculty, it is absolutely essential to make teacher hiring and evaluation top priorities.

· 9 ·

Leading Special
Education in Your School

$\mathcal{U}$nless you enter school administration with a background in special education, you will likely feel underprepared in this area. Ever since the passage of the Education for All Handicapped Children Act (PL 94-142; U.S. Department of Education, 2007) in 1975, special education laws, regulations, programs, and services in schools have expanded dramatically.

Before PL 94-142, special education services were most often limited to pullout tutoring or self-contained classes for more severe learning needs. Much less was known about how to help students with various learning difficulties succeed. In fact, back in the 1960s and early 1970s, it was not uncommon for teachers to "just do their best" with learning disabled students. Often teachers simply lowered their expectations and passed them along year to year (Kersten, 2009).

Yet once mandated by PL 94-142 and its various reauthorizations under the Individuals with Disabilities Act (IDEA), special education grew dramatically. As its knowledge base expanded, so did special education services in schools. Today, it is not uncommon for school districts to have special education classrooms that have as many adults providing assistance as there are students. Helping fuel this growth over the past forty years have been extensive state and federal special education legislation and subsequent litigation.

Special education requirements are so complex that no principal or assistant principal, especially a beginning administrator, is likely to understand every aspect. Yet building-level administrators are expected to lead their schools' special education programs. This raises an important question, especially for you as a new administrator: what do you need to know about special education if you are to lead your school's special education program and ensure compliance with federal, state, and school district special education regulations?

LEGAL MANDATES

Essential to any new administrator's success is an understanding of certain special education legal requirements. This is especially important because failing to follow legal and regulatory mandates can lead to conflicts with parents and teachers, unnecessary school district expenses, and legal proceedings.

Discussed below are several important special education legal mandates with which you should be familiar. Many of these are linked to specific deadlines, documentation requirements, and required responsibilities. Ignorance of any of these is no excuse for failure to provide services. In fact, if one of your faculty members fails to meet any of these requirements, you could find yourself apologizing to your superintendent or, even worse, meeting with your school district attorney to respond to a due process request or even a lawsuit.

LEAST RESTRICTIVE ENVIRONMENT

A fundamental requirement of PL 94-142 is that students with special needs be educated in the *least restrictive environment* (LRE). LRE is defined as follows. "Children with disabilities are to be educated, to the maximum extent appropriate, with students without disabilities. However, educational placements (and services) for students with disabilities must be consistent with their educational needs" (Beyer and Johnson 2005, 38). Under PL 94-142, it is your responsibility to stress that special-need students must be allowed to demonstrate that they can learn in the least restrictive placement.

Although this may appear self-evident, not everyone will always agree. As a result, at times you may find yourself mediating various disputes. The most common are those between parents who believe that their child would be best served in the regular classroom and faculty members pushing for a self-contained or an out-of-district placement.

As the building administrator, one of your responsibilities is to ensure that students are served in the least restrictive environment. As part of your role, you need to help faculty members understand and accept this legal requirement. Here is where you can enlist the support of other administrators and special education personnel to assist you. By being a strong advocate for least restrictive placements, you establish a common schoolwide standard while helping create a more student-centered school environment.

SPECIAL EDUCATION SERVICE ELIGIBILITY

In the United States, identified special education students are eligible for special education services from birth to age twenty-two. In most instances, it is the states, not local public school districts, that are responsible for providing services for children from birth to three.

Once children reach their third birthday, if eligible, they must be provided with appropriate special education services by public schools. Students are evaluated every three years and, if they are eligible, special education services continue until high school graduation. Students who require functional/life/job skills may receive training and support until twenty-two years of age. These students participate in graduation with their regular education peers. However, some receive certificates of completion, while others get a diploma (depending upon district practice).

PARENTAL RIGHTS

School districts are required to provide parents or guardians with notification of their parental rights annually. In addition, parents must receive a copy of the paperwork upon initial referral or at any time they request it. They must also receive notification of their rights when they or the district files a due process complaint, as well as when their child is suspended from school for more than ten days (Sraga, Engler, and Boyle, 2007). To increase the likelihood of meeting this requirement, you should designate specific individuals who are responsible for parent notification.

THE "REFERRAL CLOCK"

One mistake you cannot afford to make is failing to respond to a parent's request for an evaluation of a child. Always treat parent issues very thoroughly and ensure ample communication. When parents suspect a learning problem, they may make an assessment request in writing, by e-mail, or simply by mentioning it to you or a faculty member. The "referral clock" begins to tick the moment the parent makes the request. The school team (regular education teacher, psychologist, and any other related service providers) meets to consider the request for evaluation and completes the necessary paperwork (Sraga, Engler, and Boyle, 2007).

This does not mean, though, that a student assessment must be completed immediately. Under federal law, you must first determine whether an assessment is warranted. The parents must be notified in writing in ten school days if an evaluation is not warranted. If testing is recommended, the school team has a specified number of days to complete the assessment and develop the individualized education plan (IEP). The required number of days varies from state to state (Sraga, Engler, and Boyle, 2007).

The IEP is an extremely important document for both the student and the school district. It is a legal document that is individually developed to define the student's educational program and services (Beyer and Johnson, 2005). As the school administrator, you must ensure that it is completed accurately and appropriately within required legal deadlines. Once in place, it must be followed by staff.

You must also represent the school district during the IEP development process. You must be vigilant, so that the child receives the services required to make educational gains. Remember that the services on the IEP are not considered a menu of options from which to choose. Rather, they are required services. By being an active IEP team member, you can represent well the interests of both the child and the school district.

PARENT INVOLVEMENT

A mandatory component of the special education assessment process is parent participation. Parents are equal members of the IEP team. School administrators must ensure that parents are afforded the opportunity to discuss their children's needs and offer their personal insights. When school districts fail to allow parents meaningful involvement and do not document, in writing, their participation, they open themselves and their school districts to legal and political problems. Remember this basic legal principle: The IEP is a stand-alone document. If something is not written, it did not occur.

You should document parent participation by recording their comments in the IEP on the "additional notes" page. You are not required to implement whatever parents request, but you must show that their input was seriously considered. School personnel are required to provide parents with copies of all reports and IEP documents at the end of an IEP meeting.

PARENT REQUESTS

During your first year as an administrator, you may be approached by parents requesting that they be allowed to bring others to various meetings regarding their special education children. They may make other demands as well. Such requests usually occur when communication between the school and parents has broken down. It is imperative for you to know your rights and those of the parents in these situations.

Parents have the right to invite anyone they choose, such as friends, relatives, advocates, and attorneys, to meetings. You cannot exclude them. However, if the parents bring an attorney, you should have your school attorney represent the district, if at all possible. Even though other opinions are being expressed, the principal should maintain control over the meeting. The key is to be a proactive leader.

Also, parents may request to audiotape or videotape a meeting. If in doubt, you should discuss their request with your superintendent, who can decide if legal advice is necessary. Also, you should check your school board policy manual before allowing any recordings.

Without a policy prohibiting it, you should allow them to audiotape the session, but you should record it also. Some school attorneys advise administrators to refuse audiotaping requests if the parents have an attorney present, since this should negate the need. One complicating factor to consider is whether a parent's audiotaping request is justified because the parent has a disability. The parent may argue that because of a disability, audiotaping is necessary. If the parent provides satisfactory evidence of the need, you should approve the request.

Although the law is not explicit, generally you have the right to refuse a request to videotape because of confidentiality concerns. Requests to videotape are extremely rare.

Finally, parents who ask to visit their child's classroom generally must be permitted to do so. As the administrator, you are allowed to limit the number of visits and their length. You can insist that they make a visitation appointment. Also, you can limit them to no more than one guest at a time. However, check your board policy for any established guidelines. A sound practice is for you or a designated staff member to accompany them for the entire visit. You should take notes, which will be important later if differences of interpretation arise.

After you assume your new position, you should review any district policies related to any of the above and discuss them with appropriate administrative personnel, so that you are prepared to respond appropriately.

CLASS-SIZE AND WORKLOAD REQUIREMENTS

As a new administrator, you should be familiar with special education class-size guidelines and faculty/staff workload requirements. These can vary from state to state and, in some instances, may be district specific. Soon after you accept your position, begin to research your state's and school district's requirements.

One sure way to generate controversy in your school is to place too many students in any special education class. You want to ensure that you are familiar with any applicable legal guidelines.

You can also create conflict and legal issues by mainstreaming too many special education students into a single regular education classroom or allowing too great an age span among students in a particular class. Usually, the proportion of students in any class who have IEPs cannot exceed 30 percent (Whitten et al., 2007). What makes this a little difficult to track is the fact that any IEP student, even one receiving only minimal speech services, must be counted.

Also, you want to avoid allowing teacher caseloads to exceed your state or local school district maximum. Your teachers' contract may impose specific caseload maximums. Faculty members will be very aware of caseload limit requirements and may challenge any attempt to place additional students with them.

As a beginning administrator, you should also understand how to organize services more efficiently and effectively at no additional cost to the district. One area, in particular, where this often occurs is speech. The natural tendency of speech teachers is to schedule more rather than less speech time for their students or to service students one-on-one.

You should ensure that the number of service minutes directly aligns with the number of student goals. For example, providing an hour of speech services related to one goal is possibly excessive. However, this level of service may not be if there are three goals.

If during the IEP process you simply accept whatever service levels your faculty members recommend, you may find that you do not have adequate staffing to provide them. To avoid this trap, successful administrators become active in the scheduling process. They meet with teachers to discuss scheduling options.

Public schools are not required to provide service levels commensurate with private therapy or clinical settings. Therefore, one-on-one services are generally not provided. With tight budgets and limited teacher availability in areas such as speech, social work, physical therapy, and occupational therapy, you need to use your problem-solving skills well to identify an appropriate level of services that does not exceed available district resources.

SPECIAL EDUCATION STUDENT DISCIPLINE

School administrators at all levels deal with student discipline issues. Most become very adept at handling everything from class tardiness to drug and alcohol problems. However, in recent years, increases in special education requirements have complicated the disciplining of children with IEPs. As a beginning administrator, you will need to understand the key differences so you can respond appropriately when the need arises.

Beyer and Johnson (2005) note that students with special needs are subject to the same disciplinary consequences as regular education students under four conditions. First, the discipline problem must be minor. Second, it must relate to the school's disciplinary code. Third, the disciplinary action must apply equally to all students. Fourth, any consequence will not change the student's special education placement. Common consequences such as detentions fall into this category.

Furthermore, a student with a special need "may be suspended or expelled from school, if he or she is in possession of a gun or weapon, knowingly possesses or sells illegal drugs, or causes serious bodily injury to others, as long as the disabling condition is not the primary cause of the incident" (Beyer and Johnson, 2005, 49). However, in some states, such as Illinois, in lieu of suspension students may be placed in interim alternative education settings for up to forty-five school days.

A lengthy suspension or expulsion is considered a change in student placement. Consequently, when school districts expel students with special needs or suspend them for more than ten school days, they must hold an IEP meeting before taking any action. During the meeting, a decision must be made as to whether the student's violation was related to his or her disability, which is commonly called a "manifestation determination." You also want to note that in-school suspensions are treated the same way as out-of-school suspensions when calculating the ten-day limit (Braun, 2008).

In addition, special education students cannot be "denied a free appropriate public education due to behavior that is the direct result of a disabling condition" (Beyer and Johnson, 2005, 49.) As a result, school districts must provide services to the suspended or expelled students (Braun, 2008).

As a new administrator, a sound practice is to consult with a central-office administrator if you believe that you may need to suspend or expel a student with a special need. Because of the complexity of legal, political, and practical issues involved, you should be well prepared before taking any disciplinary action.

BEHAVIORAL INTERVENTION PLAN

Some students, because of the nature of their disabilities, require the inclusion of a behavior management plan in the IEP. In fact, students who are passive, as well as those who exhibit more aggressive behaviors, may need a behavioral intervention plan. They are designed for students whose behavior interferes with their own or other students' learning.

"A behavioral intervention plan needs to be based on a functional behavior assessment including proactive positive behavior supports and interventions" (Beyer and Johnson, 2005, 50). In other words, when developing the plan, you need to complete an assessment of what the student does well and not well, along with an analysis of why the student exhibits certain behaviors. Also, if you focus on removing a problem behavior, you must decide on the behavior to replace it.

SECTION 504

Although it is not under the special education umbrella, section 504 of the Rehabilitation Act of 1974 is often closely associated with it. All administrators, but especially those entering their first position, must have a basic understanding of 504 requirements as they relate to their schools (Braun, 2008).

Although the law has applicability beyond public education, as a school administrator, it is important to remember that you cannot discriminate against anyone with disabilities, including children and adults. Under 504, any "physical or mental impairment that substantially limits one or more of his or her life activities" must be accommodated (Beyer and Johnson, 2005, 50).

"Major life activities include caring for one's self, performing manual tasks, walking, seeing, hearing, speaking, and breathing, learning, and working" (Beyer and Johnson, 2005, 50–51). In 2009, Congress provided additional examples of general activities that are major life activities, including eating, sleeping, standing, lifting, bending, reading, concentrating, thinking, and communicating (U.S. Department of Education, 2010). Section 504 is applicable to children and adults whether or not they have a handicapping condition.

When children have a perceived disability or medical diagnosis that impacts one of the major life activities and their classroom performance, a 504 plan is necessary. As with the special education mandates discussed earlier, you should seek help from district personnel when developing and implementing any 504 plan.

Many 504 accommodations are classroom based, and teachers are required to make them under a 504 plan. For example, if an audiologist assessment finds that a student has an auditory processing problem, the 504 plan will accommodate it. This may require the teacher to check for student understanding regularly and also to provide preferential seating.

This section has reviewed many key legal mandates, many of which you will likely face as you begin your administrative career. If you follow these vigilantly, you can eliminate many unnecessary conflicts while increasing your likelihood of earning the trust and support of parents and staff.

THE PRINCIPAL'S PRIMARY ROLE IN SPECIAL EDUCATION

As a building administrator, a primary special education responsibility is to ensure that all special education mandates and guidelines are followed properly. More specifically, you will oversee the IEP process, which includes identification, placement, and regular assessment of students with special needs. Although you will ultimately be responsible for ensuring that students in your school receive the appropriate services identified in their IEPs, you can rely on special services personnel for assistance. It is sound practice to consult with special education teachers, school psychologists, and district special education coordinators shortly after you assume your position. They can guide you through the IEP process.

SPECIAL EDUCATION ELIGIBILITY

An important special education leadership responsibility is determining whether a student's learning needs require special education services. This is a crucial and, at times, difficult task.

For some disabilities, special services eligibility is fairly obvious. Physical disabilities that interfere with a student's ability to learn are easiest to identify. Other conditions are not easy to spot. Some students have difficulty learning to read and write, completing assignments, focusing in class, or interacting with adults and children. These problems may or may not require special education services but nonetheless interfere with the student's learning, as well as that of other children.

Prior to the reauthorization of IDEA in 2004, special education eligibility for students with academic learning deficits was grounded in a discrepancy model. To qualify for special education services, students were tested by school psychologists to determine if they had severe discrepancy between their achievement and their ability. Students qualified for services if, for example, their verbal achievement test scores were well below their verbal ability as measured by an industry-accepted test such as the Wechsler Intelligence Scale for Children.

However, in most school districts today, special education eligibility is no longer a function of discrepancy between achievement and ability. In fact, school psychologists no longer spend most of their time testing students for eligibility. Under IDEA, beginning in 2005, most school districts have adopted a new approach, *response to intervention* (RtI), which is a prereferral early-intervention model (U.S. Department of Education, 2007).

RtI is a regular education initiative that focuses on the use of scientifically based curricula to ensure that students have rigor in their programs. Through the use of frequent student progress monitoring and scientifically based interventions, regular education faculty members assist students in making the expected academic progress. Under RtI, the emphasis has shifted from what teachers teach to how students learn. The core of RtI is looking at how teachers deliver the curriculum. Teachers need to try an extensive number of instructional approaches before considering special education services.

Although most students respond positively to these interventions, some do not and are subsequently referred for special education services. Consequently, students for whom RtI is not effective become eligible for special education assessment.

STUDENT TRANSFERS

As a beginning administrator, you will deal with parents who have children with special education needs who transfer their children into the district. Since they are presently receiving special education services, they have active IEPs. One of your responsibilities will be facilitating determination of the appropriateness of the IEP. If you adopt the existing IEP, services are provided as specified.

If you do not to adopt the existing IEP, you have ten school days after the student enrolls to change the IEP. At this point, the district IEP process is initiated. You will discover that collecting the necessary paperwork from the prior school and assessing the student may take a while. In the meantime, you must provide comparable services to those identified in the existing IEP (Sraga et al., 2007)

Also, some parents will fail to mention that their children have been receiving services. They hope that in a new setting, their children will succeed. A way to discover whether students were actually special education eligible is to make a practice of asking students themselves if they were in any special programs in their former school.

SPECIAL EDUCATION REFERRALS

Apart from transfers, students are most often referred for assessment by parents or faculty members. In fact, most referrals originate with teachers who are struggling to help students learn. If your district has a functioning RtI process, student referrals will emerge from it. In some instances, though, they may come directly from parents. If the district decides that an evaluation is not necessary, the parent must receive written notification within ten calendar days. Nonetheless, once a referral is made, you have fourteen days to determine whether an evaluation is warranted.

INDIVIDUALIZED EDUCATIONAL PLANS

Once a decision is made to complete a student assessment, you have the option of conducting a domain meeting to discuss all areas for evaluation, parent concerns, and questions to consider. This session can be conducted by a team consisting of as few individuals as just the principal and regular education teacher. Parent consent is also required.

However, some districts require that an IEP team be convened for this initial step. As a new administrator, you will want to ensure that you have an IEP team established as soon as possible. In most instances, you will be confirming the membership of an existing team. However, if one does not exist, you should assemble an IEP team quickly, so your school can respond to any referrals in a timely manner.

The primary responsibility of the IEP team is to consider all available information and make a decision as to whether a student is special education eligible.

IEP TEAM MEMBERS

Although others may be invited to participate, IEP team members must include the following:

- The child's parents/guardians, who must receive ten days' notice of the meeting.
- A regular education teacher at the grade level of the child.
- A special education teacher at a similar grade level.
- Personnel who have conducted any assessment or provided special services. (Parents can sign a form giving permission for some specialists, such as speech teachers, not to participate.)
- The school psychologist.
- A representative of the local education agency, usually the principal or assistant principal.
- Others invited by the parents.
- The student, if fourteen years of age or older. Parents have the option of excluding the child (Sraga et al., 2007).

IEP MEETING AGENDA

One of the problems you will face is that of lengthy, inefficient IEP meetings. As the building administrator, you will be expected to lead the IEP team through the IEP process. As mentioned earlier, you should familiarize yourself as soon as is practical with all aspects of this process.

One way to reduce the length of IEP meetings is to have the psychologist meet with parents beforehand to explain testing results in a more intimate setting. However, at the IEP, you must acknowledge that data were reviewed ahead of time.

Also, parents, even highly educated ones, often feel intimidated by the IEP process, which includes a large number of professionals. Consequently, one of your administrative roles is to help the team have greater empathy with parents. Such an approach can lessen conflict and improve parent-school communication.

You should know that IEP meetings must include consideration of the following items:

- reports about the student from team members, covering such details as functional performance and standardized test results, and outside reports from parents;
- team members' perceptions of student educational needs;

- the question of eligibility for special education services;
- the student's strengths;
- the parents' vision for their child;
- related services that should be provided, such as social work, speech, physical therapy, or occupational therapy, including recommended minutes of service needed to meet goals and objectives;
- required program modifications and accommodations;
- any necessary transportation services;
- additional items such as extended school-based services, physical education modifications, assistive technology, or a functional behavior management plan;
- agreement on special education placement options, including the option of providing no special education services (Sraga et al., 2007).

As the leader of the IEP team, you are responsible for ensuring compliance with all federal, state, and local laws and guidelines. Although this may seem a little overwhelming as you begin your new role, you will understand how to meet the legal requirements after just a few meetings if you stay active in the IEP process.

ANNUAL REVIEWS

Once students begin receiving special education services, school districts must conduct annual reviews of student progress toward meeting IEP goals and objectives. Although annual reviews can occur at any time during the year, most tend to be scheduled in spring. Unfortunately, this will be one of your busiest periods. Not only will the employees feel the pressures associated with the last quarter of the school year, but students will be experiencing "spring fever," which brings increased demands on your time.

By attending annual reviews, however, you can monitor recommended service levels to ensure that they are not excessive. In fact, as the district "watchdog," you have a responsibility to ensure that service levels are appropriate and remain within both legal guidelines and available district resources.

Although principals or their assistants usually attend annual reviews, this expectation can vary widely depending upon the size of your school district and the level of administrative support. In some districts, special education directors or coordinators, rather than building administrators, may represent the district and school at annual reviews.

Participating in annual reviews is an effective way for you to maintain contact with students, parents, and teachers while ensuring that all legal requirements are met. It also helps you establish positive working relationships with parents, which can pay dividends later when conflicts arise and difficult decisions must be made.

As a new administrator, you can learn a great deal about special education, along with your district's procedures, if you choose to participate in annual reviews rather than delegate responsibility to other administrative support staff. Maybe most importantly, it is a good way to establish yourself as the school leader.

For most administrators, though, annual reviews sometimes feel like one more task to add to the ever growing list of responsibilities. These feelings will be exacerbated during your first year, when the administrative learning curve is steepest. Even though your case managers or other faculty members can manage most annual reviews, you will be a more effective leader if you choose to participate. Remember that if you are laissez-faire, you may signal a lack of support for special education. Even worse, your lack of participation may result in inappropriate services or service levels finding their way into the student's revised IEP.

To ensure that student annual reviews meet legal mandates, the following should be part of the agenda:

- Discussion of the student's progress toward meeting annual goals and objectives.
- Identification of new goals and objectives. For high school age students, the IEP must also include postsecondary goals related to education and training, employment, and possibly living skills.
- Identification of related-service minutes.
- Discussion of instructional modifications and accommodations necessary for meeting the new goals and objectives.
- Discussion of transportation, as appropriate.
- Identification of additional services that may be necessary.
- Discussion of placement options, which may include continuing the present placement or switching to a new level of service. It is possible that a recommendation to discontinue services may be made. However, before this can occur, an evaluation must be made, although this may be as simple as a review of the records (Sraga et al., 2007).

STRATEGIES FOR LEADING SUCCESSFUL IEP MEETINGS

The structure and content of IEP meetings, including annual reviews, are fairly similar from district to district. The real difference lies in how efficiently and effectively they are conducted. Their success often hinges on the leadership skills of the principal or administrator leading the meeting. Well-managed sessions not only minimize potential legal challenges but also create positive working relationships between the school and parents. Discussed below are several strategies you can use to help you navigate the IEP process successfully.

Strategy 1: Remember that your first contact with parents is critical.

One of the simplest ways to impact future relationships with parents of special education students is to set a positive tone from your first contact. You might receive calls from prospective special education parents or even someone with a child less than three years old. If you are encouraging, helpful, and responsive from the first moment you speak with them, you will already be sending the message that your school is an open, friendly place and you are there to help.

Strategy 2: Recognize that having a special education child may be a "blow" to the parents' egos.

They, or other family members, may have always done well in school. Suddenly, they have a child with special needs. Understanding their perspective and helping them appreciate their child's needs can help soften their concerns.

Strategy 3: Be aware that you may be the bearer of bad news.

Ineffective administrators avoid any potential conflict and err on the side of emphasizing the positive. This, unfortunately, creates false expectations for parents and may ultimately complicate the entire process. This is especially true at the lower grades, where anxious parents may be in denial about their children's needs. You should present yourself as low-key and friendly but also objective. It is important to keep the meeting reality based, to avoid surprises that can disrupt the process.

Strategy 4: Try to understand the parent's point of view.

Too often educators believe that they know what needs to be done and fail to consider the parent's point of view. To avoid this trap, you should sensitize your faculty members to the importance of listening fully to parents.

Strategy 5: Accept reasonable parent requests.

During the special education process, parent anxiety can be great. Conflicts can arise over any variety of issues. You may want to consider supporting parent requests, such as a slight increase in weekly social work time, even if not initially suggested by the school team. Sometimes this can facilitate the special education placement process.

Strategy 6: Treat student data as your best friend.

Administrators who focus on student data will be more successful. It is much more difficult for parents or teachers to argue against assessment and performance data that substantiate information. Too often some teachers overuse personal perceptions and emotional points to seek special education services. As the new administrator, you can set the tone for greater reliance on data, if you choose.

Strategy 7: Follow all legal mandates.

Never attempt to "fudge" the rules. One of your key responsibilities is to ensure that all legal requirements are met. This means encouraging and documenting parent involvement, meeting all legal timelines, and monitoring the thoroughness of written reports and forms. If you have limited experience in this area, you can invite another district administrator or a special education coordinator to mentor you through your first few IEP processes.

Strategy 8: Ensure that all special education meetings are businesslike.

The most efficient approach to all IEP meetings is to maintain a business-like structure and tone. Although your natural tendency may be to keep things somewhat informal, this may actually decrease meeting efficiency and contribute to emotionally laden responses. These will be exacerbated when disagreements emerge between staff, parents, and other participants.

Strategy 9: Consider holding a premeeting with key faculty members.

When you assume your new position, you may want to consider having a premeeting with faculty team members before your first few IEP meetings. Since you have yet to work with your team, you will need to get to know each other and come to a common understanding of how IEP meetings will be conducted. You can begin this process during a premeeting. These are acceptable as long as you are not making placement decisions. They can also be helpful before any IEP meeting during which you sense there may be disagreement among staff members.

Strategy 10: Assign someone to take notes.

When you are conducting an IEP meeting, it is difficult to lead the session, take notes, and complete required forms. As a beginning administrator, you will likely also lack the special education expertise to complete all documents correctly. Consequently, you should consider asking one of the team members, possibly the person who will be the student's case manager, to serve in this role. This is especially important since you will be providing parents with copies of all documents before they leave.

Strategy 11: Consider having common forms.

Always try to have the same types of forms for similar services. Rather than taking copious notes or using different forms throughout the year, a common document that can easily be completed during the meeting is preferable. This will also cut down on mistakes, including failure to complete necessary documents.

Strategy 12: Consider sending proposed student goals and objectives to parents prior to an IEP annual review.

Rather than waiting to present proposed student goals and objectives for the first time at the annual review, send them to parents beforehand. Ideally, these should be written in language parents can understand. Since parents are already familiar with their child's performance to date and understand the annual review process, you can increase the efficiency of the meetings with this extra layer of communication. Parents will be able to review the materials before the meeting and arrive better prepared to discuss them. You want to make sure that the proposed goals and objectives are clearly marked "drafts."

Strategy 13: Ensure that novice special education teachers are well prepared.

When you assume your first administrative position, you may very well have beginning special education faculty members. You cannot assume that they were prepared fully during their teacher education programs. To minimize new teacher mistakes, ask one of your veteran special education staff members to mentor the new teacher.

DISAGREEMENTS BETWEEN THE SCHOOL AND PARENTS

No matter how successful you are, sometimes you cannot avoid conflicts with the parents of special education students over their children's placements or levels of service. Such disagreements are often resolved at the school level. If not, a first step is for the IEP team to hold a resolution session without attorneys present, to attempt to resolve differences. If this is unsuccessful, the next step is a mediation session. If that is unsuccessful, the next step is a due process hearing. By law, both parents and school districts may initiate due process hearings.

As a beginning administrator, you will not be expected to lead mediation meetings or due process hearings alone. By the time a conflict reaches either of these stages, district central office and possibly special education cooperative administrators will be involved. These processes will be very time-consuming, stressful, and expensive.

You should recognize that these legal options exist to resolve disputes at the school level, if at all possible. Do not be afraid to ask for help from in-district and out-of-district administrators. If, on the other hand, you recognize that a conflict will escalate, you want to inform your central office administration as soon as possible.

SUMMARY

One of the most significant challenges you will face as a beginning administrator is providing special education leadership in your school. Administrative responsibilities associated with special education have grown dramatically over the past thirty-five years. The number of programs and services has rapidly increased. Although the sheer number of special education legal requirements and state and federal mandates today is enormous, several are particularly important for day-to-day school management.

This chapter began with a discussion of the special education legal requirements that are most essential for beginning school administrators. Discussed also was section 504 of the Rehabilitation Act of 1973, which, although not part of the special education continuum of services, has implications for school special services.

The principal's role in special education was explored. Particular emphasis was placed on providing leadership from identification of special education eligibility through IEP development to annual reviews. Strategies new administrators could use to facilitate IEP and annual reviews were offered. Also discussed was the management of differences between the school and parents over student service levels and placements.

· 10 ·

Working Smarter, Not Harder

$\mathcal{W}$hen was the last time you heard a teacher or administrator say that he or she was bored because of not having enough to do? It rarely, if ever, happens. For educators, and especially administrators, time is one of the most cherished commodities. Most administrators, and even more so new administrators, never seem to have enough hours in a day to accomplish all that needs to be done.

Yet some administrators appear less efficient and more scattered than others. The most efficient administrators always seem to be on top of the details, meet deadlines, and arrive at meetings on time. Furthermore, they have a way of projecting the appearance that they have time for you even when they do not. Others present themselves as overworked and rushed. They seem to fly into meetings late and harried. Why are they so different?

The reality is that people are very different. Everyone has personal strengths and weaknesses. A key to professional success is recognizing what you need to improve and developing skills to accommodate nonstrength areas, especially for efficiency.

MYERS AND BRIGGS

To understand why individuals, including school administrators, can be so different, it is helpful to consider the seminal work of Myers and Briggs (Myers and Briggs Foundation, 2010). Katharine Cook Briggs and her daughter Isabel Briggs Myers published the Myers-Briggs Type Indicator instrument in 1962. Based upon the work of Carl Jung, they developed a personality assessment tool designed to identify personality preferences along four continua: extrovert (E)–introvert (I); sensing (S)–intuition (N); thinking (T)–feeling (F); and judging (J)–perceiving (P) (Myers and Briggs Foundation 2010).

Their forced-choice response questionnaire is useful in identifying personality types. For example, by completing the survey, you can assess whether you tend to be more extroverted or introverted, and whether you take information in primarily through your senses or tend to focus on the "big picture," valuing insight and placing greater trust in intuition. Also, you can judge whether your natural orientation to the world is more likely to be based on organization, structure, and closure (J), or is more spontaneous, open-ended, and flexible (P). Finally, you can assess whether you are primarily a more cognitive and analytical decision maker (T), rather than one who is grounded more in feelings (F).

Those who complete the instrument not only discover their personal tendencies but also appreciate the different personality types of others. For some administrators, organization, structure, and focus are natural skills. Others revel in the world of ideas and relish uncertainty and creative thought. Neither is good or bad; they are just different (Briggs Myers, 1993).

Myers and Briggs's work is useful because it helps describe individuals' personality types. Once you recognize how different people are, you will also begin to understand why some individuals feel more comfortable in certain settings than others. However, you also must recognize that certain personal tendencies are more associated with administrative success than are others.

The reality for your success as a new administrator is that you must be structured, organized, and focused even if your personality tendencies are quite different. If you do not adjust, you can quickly undermine your personal success. If "school things" are not well managed, the result is usually confusion and discontent among stakeholders.

As a beginning administrator, you may want to take some time to assess your personal tendencies. The Myers-Briggs materials, which include the instrument and scoring guides, are available either in print or online. You can use the assessment results to gain valuable insights about yourself. Once you recognize your personality preferences, you can concentrate on identifying your personal strengths and personality preferences and also adjust for any weaknesses.

STRATEGIES TO WORK SMARTER, NOT HARDER

If you are a naturally focused and well-organized person, you will not face some of the leadership challenges other personality styles do. However, no matter what your personal tendencies, you can increase your productive work time by eliminating many of the inefficiencies that plague some administrators. You will discover that as you learn to improve your personal efficiency, you will find valuable time that you can use to contribute to your leadership success. Below are several recommended strategies to help you work smarter, not harder.

Strategy 1: Handle mail well.

Although more and more communication is electronic, school administrators still receive a substantial amount of mail. The longer you are an administrator and the more contact you have with vendors and various organizations, the greater the volume of daily mail you will receive.

Opening your mail can be a great time-waster. Your goal should be to open only mail you really need to see. A first step to mail efficiency is asking your office staff to sort through it before you even see it. With some guidance from you, they can learn to screen out a substantial portion of your "junk mail." They can also redirect those items addressed to you but actually intended for someone else.

One word of caution is in order: if you overdelegate, you run the risk of missing important communications. A good approach, especially for beginning administrators, is to encourage your office staff to let you make the final decision on anything about which they are unsure.

For those items that remain, you must resist the temptation to open every piece. Depending upon your personality type, this may be very difficult. Do you really need to see the promotional flyer sent by a custodial supply firm? Remember that these vendors rarely send something only to the principal. It is more likely that they have sent the same promotional piece to others in your school and the district. There is rarely any reason for you to open a marketing piece and forward it to someone else.

When handling mail, another good time-saving strategy is to discard any obvious presorted, generic mail directly into the trash receptacle. Unless you are familiar with the sender or looking for a particular piece, you will never miss it. This technique will discourage you from keeping items that you will find yourself looking at again later. By utilizing these simple techniques, you can save fifteen minutes a day or more. At the same time, you will reduce the paper clutter apparent in some administrators' offices, which also must be managed at some point.

Strategy 2: Manage electronic communication efficiently.

Although electronic communication has had a positive impact on personal and organizational efficiency, it can also be a major contributor to inefficiency. On the one hand, you can use websites and software to save time. For example, rather than "playing phone (or e-mail) tag" to schedule a meeting, you could use Web-based software such as Doodle. With Doodle, you create an online calendar of available meeting dates and times and invite participants to indicate the days they are available. In a quick glance, both you and the participants can see when everyone is available.

Products such as these are readily available. The difficulty is finding out that they exist. To do so, you may want to watch for workshops in your area on using technology for management efficiency. You can also network with other administrators and technology support personnel to research what they use and what they recommend. Perhaps the most effective tactic is to identify administrators in your area who have the reputation of being technology savvy. These individuals tend to gravitate toward technology applications and usually have a good sense of the latest options available. They will be able to steer you in the right direction.

On the other hand, technology may interfere with efficiency. Do you know administrators who spend all day glued to their desks working at their computers? They always seem busy, but are they? One of the issues surrounding inefficient administration is your personal definition of productivity. Some define productivity as being constantly busy. However, being busy is not necessarily linked to productivity.

These administrators may view interacting with electronic media as productive work. It may be, but it also may not be. As with any decision you make on how to use your time, your productivity is better measured by what you accomplish than your level of "busyness."

Inefficient administrators waste a substantial portion of their day checking and writing unnecessary e-mails and visiting extraneous websites. A classic example is the administrator who sends e-mails that result in a constant flow of group e-mails back and forth. These e-mail conversations often digress into humorous interchanges during which everyone feels compelled to comment. Yes, you will look busy, but is what you are doing productive? Before electronic communication, this could not occur as easily as it does now.

Another time-waster can be "reply to all," which is grossly overused. When administrators respond regularly to entire groups, they create unnecessary communication. If, for example, your superintendent e-mailed the administrators to confirm whether they would attend a meeting, and everyone responded with "reply to all," would you not feel compelled to open each one "just in case"? Often, the response is "I will be there." A way to improve efficiency for yourself and your staff is to point out why this response can waste time. You should encourage others to use "reply to all" sparingly.

"Reply to all" can also be damage your reputation. Have you ever heard of someone who accidentally e-mailed an entire group a response that was intended for an individual? Overuse of this response option can increase its accidental use. Do not use "reply to all" unless it is appropriate.

School attorneys today also recommend increased face-to-face or written communication over electronic communication. When you use electronic communication, you provide easy access to what you write because these are subject to Freedom of Information Act requests.

Finally, how you manage your e-mail mailbox can have a substantial impact on your available time. One useful approach is to ensure that you make full use of your school district's "junk e-mail" software system. If you find that certain unwanted e-mails are slipping through, speak to your technology support personnel.

Also, consider becoming a "delete junkie." Some administrators struggle with hitting the delete button. Instead, they either create subfolders to store e-mails or wind up with screen after screen of dormant e-mails in the in-box. To counter this tendency, consider adopting the following practices.

- Whenever you open your e-mail, go through unopened items and delete as many as possible before opening them. Think for a moment. Is that daily Orbitz vacation special really something you need to read? After you get into the "delete" habit, you will start to feel good every time you clear a substantial number of unnecessary e-mails from your screen.
- Create a subfolder called "archive" in which you place only those e-mails that you absolutely need to save. For example, if you are having a problem with a current employee or parent, you may want to save all communications for some time. By moving these to the archive file, you can store them for future deletion without cluttering your current in-box screen. This will allow you to delete new e-mails more efficiently since you will not have to revisit as many e-mails each time.
- Make a point of cleaning up your "in," "delete," and "sent" boxes every Friday before you leave.
- Check your e-mail sometime on Sunday evening with the express purpose of deleting as many items as possible. All those unwanted e-mails that regularly appear can be cleaned out. When you arrive at the office on Monday, you will minimize the distractions created by long lists of unopened e-mails.

Strategy 3: Use social networking appropriately.

It seems that new methods of communicating are regularly emerging. Three of the most recent are blogging, Twittering, and creating a Facebook page. Also, LinkedIn, a network of professional contacts, is commonly used by leaders in education and business. Under the right circumstances, social networking is effective for creating professional forums. However, social networking tools can also lead to potential problems for school administrators if not used well. These problems can be minimized if you understand how to use them properly.

You should avoid using Twitter during the work day. Twitter "tweets" are limited to 140 characters and are used primarily to provide a running commentary of activity. If you have something to communicate during work time, either a phone call or e-mail is preferable.

Blogging takes personal commitment to use effectively. Individuals who blog generally post their positions on a blogging website and invite others to comment. To use blogging well, you must regularly record comments and also respond to others. Blogs are difficult to sustain. If you are not able to monitor your blog closely, you may want to use other forms of communication to solicit information.

Facebook probably carries the greatest risk for you as an administrator. Although it is useful for establishing contacts with others and keeping people up to date about you, it can open you up to potential professional dangers. Whatever you add to your Facebook page, will, in likelihood, remain there for years to come. You must expect that employers, parents, staff members, and others will see it, even if you think the material is private. One thoughtless inclusion could haunt you for years to come. You want to use it judiciously.

Also, a Facebook page allows other to criticize you electronically and publicly. Consider for a moment whether you want to create a public website through which disgruntled parents could post negative comments about you.

Strategy: 4: Recognize appropriate and inappropriate uses of e-mail.

Ask yourself if you really need to respond to every e-mail from someone with whom you are communicating. Although it is common courtesy to let someone know you have received a message, at what point do you stop thanking each other back and forth? Do you thank correspondents back because they thanked you for responding to them? This might seem silly on the surface, but this can become an unnecessary time-waster. As you work with others, gradually decide how you can minimize these back-and-forth e-mails yet have confidence that what had to be communicated was.

Also, do not feel compelled to acknowledge all electronic communication. Do you find yourself the recipient of constant humorous e-mails that you either do not want or only care to access occasionally? If you are, remember that responding to these only encourages more. In addition, do not be afraid to let a friend or colleague know that you are not interested in receiving them. You can spend unnecessary time just deleting them, even if you do not read any.

Finally, you should minimize your use of personal e-mail at work. Once you use your school computer for personal e-mails, they can be accessed by others at some point, especially if a problem emerges.

Strategy 5: Manage paper.

As with electronic communication, some administrators have difficulty with paper management. Have you ever walked into someone's office and observed piles of paper everywhere? If you ask such people how they find anything, they typically respond that they know where everything is and can find anything they want quickly. This may or may not be true.

The reality is that people, as highlighted by Myers and Briggs (2010), have very different personalities. Some struggle with throwing anything away. If you are this type of person, you cannot completely change your style. However, you can find ways to be more efficient.

Paper hoarding results in two issues for a beginning administrator. A messy office sends the message that you are disorganized, whether you are or are not. Second, clutter almost always creates inefficiencies that waste valuable time. If your natural tendency is to be a saver, you may want to consider the suggestions below.

- Never touch a piece of paper more than once if you do not have to. This is easy to say but difficult to do. However, if you begin to develop this mind-set, you will be more likely to discard unnecessary items.
- Identify what files your office staff can maintain and get into the habit of expecting them to store copies.
- Avoid the temptation to add filing space to your office. The more file cabinets and drawers you have, the greater the likelihood that you will fill them.
- Think in terms of one copy, not multiple copies. Too often, inefficient administrators make multiple copies of everything. This can become automatic. Remember that you will be "greener" and decrease paper usage if you limit copying.
- Try not to print e-mails at all.
- Maximize open desktop space. A mind-set you want to develop is that of keeping a certain percentage of your desktop visible. By thinking "open," you can train yourself to be more efficient.

Strategy 6: Create a yearlong planning calendar.

For a first year administrator, a yearlong planning calendar can be very useful. After you accept your position, start to build a month-by-month calendar in which you include school, district, and community events; meeting dates; special activities; due dates; and major organizational tasks. Also include anticipated dates to begin working on projects, as well as important time-sensitive deadlines for various tasks. As the year progresses, you can add to your calendar. This will help you visualize what needs to be done while allowing you to focus on the broader picture. You can also use it as a planning tool for the following school year.

Strategy 7: Dedicate certain times of the day for particular responsibilities.

One characteristic of inefficient individuals is that they have difficulty organizing and maintaining their activity focus. They begin one task and suddenly become distracted by another. Some waste precious time shifting between activities, which might even mean leaving one work space for another. Still others have trouble focusing on the most appropriate time to deal with something, and because of this inefficiency, it takes longer to do it. They would be better off addressing it later.

If you find that time management might be an area for improvement, consider the following suggestions.

- Try to either arrive early or stay late, depending upon your preference, to focus on nonimmediate items. Some administrators will tell you that they reserve a period of time daily when most teachers are not there to write reports, plan activities, return nonessential phone calls, and complete paperwork. The more you can reduce the interruptions when accomplishing these types of tasks, the less often you will have to "begin over."
- Prioritize what needs to be accomplished. Begin your day by differentiating between high and low priorities. Some administrators create priority lists, which they modify as the day unfolds.
- Do not avoid unpleasant tasks. It is easy to do what you enjoy and procrastinate about what you do not. The problem is that you will keep revisiting the unpleasant tasks over and over. Each time you do, you waste valuable time and energy.
- Turn off the "new e-mail" sound and limit the number of times you check your e-mail daily. If you let others know why you are doing this, they will not expect an instantaneous response. If they really need to talk with you, they can work through your office staff.

- Identify specifically what task or what part of a task you will accomplish at a particular time, and focus on it to completion.
- Do not be afraid to close your office door for some period of time. You will not earn a reputation as a "closed-door administrator" if you tell others why you do this. If you vary the time of day, length, and frequency, this short, focused session will help you stay on the task at hand.
- Delegate more. Most inefficient administrators have to have their hands in everything and cannot seem to delegate. By letting others take responsibility for some of what needs to be accomplished, you empower them and free up valuable time.

Strategy 8: Conduct more efficient and effective meetings.

Did you ever sit in on a committee meeting that wandered endlessly without focus and structure? Did committee members tend to wander to unrelated topics, even while someone was talking? Meetings are endemic to the work of schools. A large amount of time is spent meeting with groups around any number of issues. Conducting meetings well can have a huge impact on everyone's time, including that of the school leader.

By and large, teachers, staff, and parents want to be and should be involved in much of what happens at the school. However, this does not mean sitting in unproductive sessions. These discourage involvement rather than create momentum. As the leader, you are expected to conduct a variety of meetings smoothly and efficiently, while allowing participants to feel involved.

Conducting a meeting well is not a chance event. Administrators who make meetings productive understand how to do so. As a beginning administrator, you can garner some immediate support and encourage active, productive participation if you run a meeting well. Listed below are several suggestions for conducting efficient and effective school meetings.

- Never call a meeting without a specific, defined purpose. Just inviting others to meet does not mean you are being collaborative, nor does this approach equate with increased stakeholder support.
- Always prepare an agenda, which is preferably distributed before the meeting. If appropriate, encourage others to suggest modifications or additional items ahead of time.
- Begin by articulating goals and expected outcomes for the meeting. Too often, the purpose of a meeting is vague. For example, if the meeting is to identify the procedures for the upcoming parent-conference

night, you should define this goal and discuss the role of the committee members before you begin.

- Utilize a meeting management style that allows everyone to participate
  and discourages dominance of the discussion by one or two individuals. In some instances, you may actually have to have a more rigid
  participation structure, such as calling on individuals in turn based
  on when they raise their hands. You will want to think this through
  before the meeting and discuss both the approach and the reason for
  it with the group before the meeting begins.
- As individuals are talking, take some notes to begin to provide structure for the discussion. You should identify key points and issues that
  you can use later to summarize the committee work. Better yet, make
  sure that you keep a copy of the notes for future reference.
- Do not hesitate to interrupt the discussion at various intervals to summarize what has occurred. You can start by saying something such as,
  "At this point, let me summarize the key points I have heard made."
  After this, you can solicit reactions before identifying where to move
  the discussion. By summarizing the discussion, you refocus the committee and begin to move toward closure.
- Always end a meeting with a summary of where the group is relative
  to the purpose you identified up front. This will provide a direction for
  the next meeting or additional actions.
- Depending on the meeting, you may want to follow up with a written
  summary. This is especially important when specific organizational
  items are discussed or important decisions made.

SUMMARY

This chapter has focused on the use of time for efficiency. Because time is
such a precious commodity for all stakeholders, the most successful school
leaders use their time and the time of others effectively.

One key to administrative success is recognizing that individuals are
inherently different. This chapter began with a discussion of why individuals, including administrators, are so unique. It included a discussion of the
Myers and Briggs personality assessment tool. Once you understand others'
personality tendencies, as well as your own, you can begin to make the accommodations that are necessary to increase efficiency.

Finally, a series of strategies was offered, which beginning administrators should consider to help them work smarter, not harder. Practical time-
saving tips were included in the discussion. By focusing on working smarter
rather than harder, you can enhance your leadership success.

Closing Thoughts

School administration can be one of the most exciting, rewarding, and important positions in education. If you want to have a broader influence on both student learning and school improvement, you will find that nothing can be more satisfying than leading a school. Although, at times, you will find that school leadership can be very stressful and the workload demanding, you will also feel the exhilaration that is inherent in effective school administration.

Although school leadership success requires enthusiasm, initiative, and a positive attitude, these are not enough. Rather, they are the prerequisites to success. Effective school leadership is far more complex. Success is built on a blend of knowledge, leadership skills, and personal qualities that, in some instances, are learned during your early years in education. They are enhanced through graduate program studies and honed during the first few years in administration.

An important first step toward building a career in school administration is maximizing the impact of your early years in education. Many of those who have ultimately become highly effective school leaders recognized that this time was an opportunity to learn as much about teaching and school management as possible. As teachers, they experimented with what they were learning in professional development and their educational leadership programs. They took the initiative to seek out leadership experiences within their school districts, to help them test their skills in a sheltered environment.

In addition, they recognized that their educational leadership programs provided more potential for their personal development than merely moving up on the salary schedule. Rather, they treated their educational leadership preparation as a learning opportunity. Course work, readings, and collegial interactions, as well as clinical and internship experiences, all provided valuable insights into the world of school leadership. During their administrative preparation programs, they were able to test their own leadership skills before ever accepting their first administrative positions.

This book, *Stepping into Administration: How to Succeed in Making the Move*, has explored the journey from preparing for an administrative career through the initial administrative year. It was built on the conviction that a substantial portion of leadership effectiveness can be learned and that preparation can enhance a new administrator's initial success.

As a consequence, if you have certain knowledge, skills, and experiences before you accept your first administrative position, you can substantially increase your chances for success. By understanding what successful administrators know and do and avoiding the mistakes associated with those who fail, you can successfully transition from the classroom to a school leadership position and truly make a difference in the lives of children.

References

American Association for Employment in Education. (2009). The job market today: Interpreting the 2008 educator supply and demand research. *2010 Job Search Handbook for Educators* 43, 44–46.

Beyer, B. M., and Johnson, E. S. (2005). *Special programs and services in schools.* Lancaster, PA: Pro>Active.

Blase, J. R., and Blase, J. (1998). *Handbook of instructional leadership: How effective principals promote teaching and learning.* Thousand Oaks, CA: Corwin.

Braun, B. A. (2008). *Illinois school law survey* (10th ed.). Springfield, Ill.: Illinois Association of School Boards.

Briggs Myers, I. (1993). Introduction to type: A guide to understanding your results on the Myers-Briggs type instrument (5th ed.). Revised by L. Kirby and K. Myers. Palo Alto, CA: Consulting Psychologists Press.

Bureau of Labor Statistics. (2009). *Occupational out look handbook, 2009–2010 edition.* Washington, DC: U.S. Department of Labor. Available from www.bls.gov/oco/ocos007.htm.

Collins, J. (2001). *Good to great: Why some companies make the leap . . . and others don't.* New York: HarperCollins.

Darling-Hammond, L., LaPointe, M., Meyerson, D., Orr, M., and Cohen, C. (2007). *Preparing school leaders for a changing world: Lessons from exemplary leadership development programs.* Stanford: Stanford Educational Leadership Institute, Stanford University.

Davis, S., Darling-Hammond, L., LaPointe, M., and Meyerson, D. (2005). *School leadership study: Developing successful principals.* Stanford: Stanford Educational Leadership Institute, Stanford University.

DuFour, R. (2007). In praise of top-down leadership. *The School Administrator*, November 1, 38–42.

Kachur, D., Stout, J., and Edwards, C. (2010). *Classroom walkthroughs to improve teaching and learning.* Larchmont, NY: Eye on Education.

Kersten, T. (2006). Principal selection processes: Best practice for superintendents. In F. L. Dembowski and L. K. Lemasters (eds.), *Unbridled spirit: Best practices in educational administration*, 363–73. Lancaster, PA: Pro>Active.

———. (2008). Teacher hiring practices: Illinois principals' perspectives. *The Educational Forum 72*(4), 355–68.

———. (2009). *Taking the mystery out of Illinois school finance* (2nd ed.). Houston: NCPEA Press.

Leithwood, K., Seashore, L. K., Anderson, S., and Wahlstrom, K. (2004). *How leadership influences student learning*. New York: Wallace Foundation.

Marshall, K. (2009). Mini observations. *Education Week*, February 4, 24–25.

Marzano, R. J., Waters, J. T., and McNulty, B. A. (2005). *School leadership that works: From research to results*. Alexandria, VA: Association for Supervision and Curriculum Development.

Murphy, J. (2002). Reculturing the profession of educational leadership: New blueprints. In J. Murphy (ed.), *The educational challenge: Redefining leadership for the twenty-first century*, 65–82. Chicago: National Society of Education.

Myers and Briggs Foundation. (2010). *My MBTI personality type*. Retrieved from www.myersbriggs.org/my-mbti-personality-type/.

Schmoker, M. (2001). *The results fieldbook: Practical strategies for dramatically improved schools*. Alexandria, VA: Association for Supervision and Curriculum Development.

Sraga, A. T., Engler, T. E., and Boyle, D. M. (2007). *Defensible IEPs*. Oak Brook, IL: Sraga, Engler, and Boyle, LLC.

U.S. Bureau of Labor Statistics. (2009). *Occupational outlook handbook: 2008-09 edition*. Washington, DC: U.S. Department of Labor.

U.S. Department of Education. (2007). Archived: A twenty-five year history of the IDEA. Special Education and Rehabilitative Services. Retrieved from www.ed.gov/policy/speced/leg/idea/history.html.

———. (2010). Frequently asked questions about Section 504 and the education of children with disabilities. Office for Civil Rights. Retrieved from www2.ed.gov/about/offices/list/ocr/504faq.html.

Whitten, P. S., Kriha, D. L., Smith, J. A., O'Keefe, C. F., and Wernz, J. F. (2007). *Special education update: Including revocation and consent, service animals and allergies, school visitors and the 70/30 rule*. Chicago: Franczek Radelet PC.

Zepeda, S. J. (2007). *Instructional supervision: Applying tools and concepts* (2nd ed.). Larchmont, NY: Eye on Education.

About the Author

Thomas A. Kersten is an associate professor of Educational Leadership at Roosevelt University in Chicago and Schaumburg, Illinois. He has served as an Illinois school administrator for twenty-eight years during which he was an assistant principal, elementary school principal, middle school principal, assistant superintendent, and superintendent.

Breinigsville, PA USA
31 July 2010
242726BV00001B/2/P